Soul Manifestos and Pieces of Joy

by Steve Thorp

Soul Manifestos and Pieces of Joy

Third print edition, ©2018

Cover and illustrations by Ruth Thorp
www.ruththorpstudio.co.uk

ISBN: 978-0-9928647-1-2

Published by Raw Mixture Publishing
The Granary, Middle Tancredston,
Haverfordwest, Pembrokeshire, SA62 5PX
www.rawmixture.co.uk

Printed by Gomer Press, Wales
on papers from sustainable sources.

Contents

Part 6: On being free and crumbling

Part 7: Small things and dangerous words

Introduction

If you've found your way to this book, I thank you for your interest. Something might have drawn you: the title, theme or fortunate chance. Whatever your reasons, I hope you find something here to make you think, reflect or see things a little differently.

At the heart of the matter are three ideas woven through these small soul manifestos and pieces of joy:

1 *The ecological and social crises we face in our times;*
2 *A secular idea of soul as a lifelong force within each one of us;*
3 *The power of imagination in telling new stories of our being.*

I am suspicious of grand visions and theories, but trust imagination and simplicity as tools for good. Some of the people I most admire give small beauties to the world, and live their life with small rhythms and patterns. Here, I have tried to write of a simple, grounded intelligence, and of ways we can work together to integrate such small wisdoms into a practical activism for the future.

This book is not a self help book – or rather not one of those that promises to change your life. You alone can make a change, and this will come only when you are ready and your life circumstances allow. And the wider changes that are needed will come only when our species awakens to the social and ecological realities of our existence on this planet at the beginning of the twenty-first century.

This book does not claim that you can be happy by thinking positively or dealing with some past difficulty from childhood. If you are someone who sees how the world we humans have created is crumbling, then you are unlikely to believe you can become happy with such a short-term fix. 'Happiness', in any case, is hardly an appropriate response to a crumbling world. My sense is that we need to draw upon a wider, more nuanced, emotional repertoire to engage more fully with the human and non-human ecosystems we live within.

The book contains a series of short manifestos, essays and meditations on the new assumptions we might need for our future. Each piece stands alone, but together they may coalesce into a gentle, intuitive polemic that seeps into the consciousness.

If the pieces in this book are about self-help at all, it is the kind that takes a lifetime. They are written about how we might live our lives with depth and soul, and how we might respond collectively to the world we live in; grounded in an engagement with our material world, rather than reaching for secrets in the stars.

So, these small manifestos are written for wonder, wisdom, joy, love, openness and engagement, and for the common-wealth, common good and the good earth. And they are written against oppression, destruction, ignorance, literalism, certainty, determinism and the hypocritical justifications for continuing on the same path we have been walking down blindly for the past century or two.

Steve Thorp, Pembrokeshire, 2014.

Part 1
Soul manifestos

Secularity

I'd like to defend emotion against the benefactor of spirit for,
feeling as we do, we are not part of your constituency –
nor does wonder (the best of emotions) belong to you.
Beauty, therefore, is neither barbaric nor the function of the eternal
(though the blank, hollow-eyed version is seen regularly in bulletins).

On the park bench, meanwhile, the nominal sceptic sits in the rain,
staring into a mazy, bloodshot sky, showing a subtle appreciation of
osmosis and a Spartan denial of the oligarchy of faith.

So I'd like to defend random variance, quirky, stickleback foresight and
mortality and, in doing so, fly a tattered flag, not in prayer, but in reverence
to quasars, hummingbirds, river dolphins and the microscopic generalities
that created this poem which, in wishing you well on the journey,
I'd like to dedicate to your unfolding, unnoticed, neglected soul.

Ordinary times

"The pattern of ordinary life, in which so much stays the same from one day to the next, disguises the fragility of its fabric".
(Paul Kingsnorth and Dougald Hine, 2009)[1]

This feels like an ordinary time. The Spring weather in Pembrokeshire is bright and balmy – the seas warming. Each day, as we drive over the hills, the sea unfolds in the distance. We shop when we need to and I cut wood to feed the fire. It feels simple enough, yet behind it all, storm clouds are looming. This existence is embedded in the fragility of modern life that Paul Kingsnorth and Dougald Hine refer to in their elegant and ferocious '*Dark Mountain Manifesto*'.

Winter here is especially stormy, and that is its charm. We always know that Spring will come, the flowers bursting out on the headlands in May. Yet the storm brewing behind this fragile, ordinary life may be a hurricane we will all have to face. When it hits there may be no calm and mellow re-birth to follow.

We know in our bones, most of us, that the lifestyle of consumerism we have been encouraged to live is unsustainable. This makes our lives far from ordinary. Over the past two centuries, the drive towards global consumption has led to barren landscapes, fragmented communities and disconnected individuals.

One psychological upshot of the centuries of fire, steel, concrete and plastic is a deep despair, carried within us, at the loss of connection with our planet.[2] However we only have to walk a headland, river bank or forest to get a hint of what is truly, wonderfully ordinary. It is remarkable that this connection with our world is still alive inside us, despite the efforts of generations of industrialists, politicians and their apologists with their spoil, spill and double-speak.

Our psychological 'therapy culture' can be seen as another way of civilising us; keeping us enclosed in our ordinary lives. Whilst we are helped to manage, cope and sometimes heal through 'proven' therapeutic interventions, the dimension of despair located in our disconnection from the world is seldom acknowledged.

We are not one-dimensional creatures, programmed to respond in predictable ways. Each of our characters has been 'over-determined': emerging from a myriad of influences that coalesce uniquely in every one of us.[3] And between the layers of each self, lies the metaphorical energy of 'soul'. Through its mediation, we derive our capacity for wonder, imagination, connection and joy: necessary counterpoints to the bleak, human givens – despair, isolation, meaninglessness, loss and conflict – that can taint our lives.

In times of crisis, many things crumble. However, two things always flower and flourish: the creative human spirit and the natural soul of the world that arises from our wild, beautiful planet. Existential knowledge of the challenges we face robs us of the comfort of certainty and meaning, yet frees us to be more fully human: to face anxiety and fear and embrace joy and fulfilment, as the scales of our nature are balanced.

This, then, is a manifesto of the soul: a psychological, spiritual and material re-balancing of the world within and without – so we can start to do something that makes a difference.

A phenomenology of uncertainty

What will be the phenomenology of a manifesto of the soul?

The psychology of the soul is of depth, authenticity and calling. Its phenomenology is watchful and subtle, concerned with things that last, not short-term expediency. However, there is also a need for a renewed activism of mind, body and earth. Honesty, hard thinking and good anger – well targeted – are required.

Soul asks us to be willing to live with what emerges within and between us. It is about love – yet this intimate, gentle position is not sufficient in itself. We can get tangled up in its deep introversions, losing ourselves in the search for healing, spirit, relationship and 'self'. So the ecological and social imperatives in our world provide a necessary counterbalance, asking that each soul is unfolded within the earth's natural, connected beauty.

To defend earth against humanity, we need erudite, analytical knowledge of its patterns and rhythms. This, in turn, requires courage to stand against those of our own kind who continue the destruction. It requires a willingness to embrace a wildness inside us and to go beyond the pale; to be lovers of small things and champions of the world's non-human 'citizenship'.

This is a complex challenge, for the habits of our daily lives seem to give us little choice but to go along with what is accepted as 'normal'. We can opt out of civilisation, of course, but can then find ourselves embroiled in the self delusion of gestural, lifestyle politics. We risk losing human connection if we reject the humanity of those whose political and economic views we do not share, and in doing so we demonise their behaviour and their person-hood.

Positions of certainty are always dangerous and self-defeating. In the end, the basic requirement of soul is to live with imagination, engagement and uncertainty. If the human world is to be redeemed, we will need the creativity that emerges from the depths of our imagination. From wherever they appear, our truest insights must lie at the heart of this rich 'unpsychology' of wildness, gentleness, anger, watchfulness and activism.

Soul-making recognises that poetry, economics, science, politics and spirit all emerge from the same animal mind. Imagination, therefore, is the warp to ecology's weft, weaving new stories and creations that can form the basis of a new culture of hope.

Twenty-first century soul

Everything we humans mean, say and do is psychological. *Psyche* is not just about mind, but body and world too, and all experience passes through this prism – colouring each moment, sense and occurrence. *Psyche* frames objectivity through inevitable subjectivity. No matter how much we try to explain or strive for sanity, an unpredictable riot of wild experience floods through.

We cannot push it away. It does not depend on permission, proof or social convention. This force, we call soul.

Soul bubbles up in everything we do. Deny it and it comes back in archetypal forms to feed violence and hatred. Accept it literally and it is fixed in spiritual dogmas that are wrapped around the human experience. However, it does not matter whether we accept soul or not, it will have its way, pushing into our lives somehow and some day. Throughout our life, this something we experience as soul guides us as a force and direction.

Yet our civilisation has lost soul. If our fractured, cultural world has a personality, it is that of a searcher no longer willing to seek and strive. Nowadays, our destinations must be reached, secrets known, goals achieved – and quickly. Everyone must be happy and fulfilled – and now.

Ambiguity, a life's work, a lasting marriage, a civilisation that has long-term vision and imagination, a planet that can sustain its lifeforms – none of these slow virtues seem comprehensible to many of us, with our 'civilised' minds.

The modern soul gets sicker with each tragedy we witness through our hi-definition screens. Each new star that rises in this cultural firmament is extinguished. In the way of a gladiatorial contest we put our thumbs down to imagination.

We condemn our souls to death, yet still yearn for wonder and transcendence. We look in the wrong places, and soul remains largely unacknowledged. Yet soul is as close to us as the grass beneath our feet, and a great deal more accessible than the fame and riches, self-fulfilment and happiness we are urged to wish for.

A soulful approach to our fractured world asks that we learn to recognise and love our fractured souls.

No other way to healing is possible or necessary.

The making of a soul

The most joyful task in life is soul-making.

It is an old-fashioned project, based on wisdom, curiosity, surrender, fealty and duty. At the same time, it is a wild making. Soul-making is not an individual task – it must be mutual and collective. To be 'soul-ful', we start to recognise the ways in which our souls and selves emerge from the world, as well as from within our deep minds.

Soul is the deepest part of us humans. It is always manifest, felt most when we are fully living and are going with the grain of our calling and character. It is in the subtle connections we have with the world – so that when we walk out, wide-eyed, our soul is constantly being re-made.

Soul is integral and inherent, something from inside that we are also part of. It is the *"best part of the personality wherever it appears"*,[4] and the 'acorn' from which we grow.[5] It is the calling that holds our potential: metaphorically, the story of our lives. Soul is also to be found in the stiff task of facing our shadows, and in our endeavours to prevent destructive fantasies being played out in the world.

Soul-making is about finding the balance between duty, temperance and belonging on the one hand, and freedom, expression and abandonment on the other. The joy of a soul being made is there when we are curious, playful and mischievous. It is there in our love and learning, and our solidarity and activism.

As a tradition, soul-making is introspective, self-analytical and self-compassionate. It is mindful of the shadows which lie inside us.

It is a poetic, philosophical and creative moulding. Yet it is also a contemporary project, much needed to develop the minds we will need to meet the challenges of the century.

Life is wild and unpredictable. The human world is in desperate need of people who can engage with the big issues facing us – the threats of climate change, scarcity and conflict – and who have the courage to inhabit the shamanic spaces at the edge of wilderness.

This soul is as secular as it is religious – as mortal and material as it is eternal and spiritual. Our legacy after our death (evoked in Irvin Yalom's poignant idea of 'rippling'[6]) is in how our wisdom, virtues and achievements live on in the soulful memories others have of us. Our soul's emergence depends on the integrity and courage we bring to our unfolding over a lifetime.

We don't need to throw out the soul baby out with the religious bathwater. Soul – this collective, existential energy – is revealed through our slow striving for knowledge, and in the illumination of our dark corners. The ultimate concern of the soul activist is how to keep alive the innermost being of humankind in this beautiful and perilous world.

Soul in the world

When a person or a culture loses soul, they are in deep trouble. If we turn from soul, deny its influence and live with an illusion that humans are masters of our destiny, then we are heading for a fall.

This is what has happened to our culture in the 'post-modern' age. Yet even as we have turned our faces from profound truth, the soul still asks that we become aware of our calling, and realign ourselves with the positive forces in our personality that shape us moment by moment.

If we are lucky, we will see the grist of our soul in the world. We might catch a glimpse of it as it works in us throughout our time on earth. We then have a chance, like a potter shapes clay, to mould and carve our selves with subtlety and care. However, it can be enough just to be in the moment – to tune into our body, mind, emotions, behaviours and imagination.

"It helps", wrote James Hillman, *"to regard soul as an active intelligence, forming and plotting each person's fate."* [7]

At times, we might mistake soul-making for a journey with a destination. This misses the truth that soul is constantly unfolding, always present in essence. Perhaps soul-making might be more accurately described as soul-revealing? Soul bubbles up in us, takes us by surprise, through poetic images that spontaneously emerge.

Soul also emerges in our connections with others and in the ways we can change our world. In this deep process, our life experiences recycle into a constellation of the self, constantly reconstructing what it means to be 'me'. In this sense, a soul is never fully made – it is always a work in progress. This recognition can be profoundly joyful. All we may need to do is notice.

Taking such a long-game approach removes the anxious striving inherent in new-age personal and spiritual development projects. More often than not, in following these paths, we seek quick answers and short-term transformation, based on the illusion that we have it within our power to change ourselves through conscious thought.

The truth of the matter is that (as James Hillman might have it) we grow down into the world in ways that can often seem destined;[8] and (as Malcolm Gladwell suggests) our success and impact in the world can be as much about chance and circumstance as something we make happen.[9]

In the end, destiny is not a destination or a determination, but a mythical force from within and without. It is about calling, circumstance and context, and most easily followed when we clear away the undergrowth. It is about living with what we have.

Night is soul time

I am drawn to the night – even as I know its fears. The trees, shadowed by moonlight through the skylight, carry something of my essence. As I watch their dance, I am led to sleep. In dreamtime, the soul has its playtime; but even when we are awake, the night is the soul's time.

In daytime, the rational mind and ego do something to the soul. They try to pin it down to a structure or belief, or deny its existence with science. In the dark, the soul knows its truth: that it is the connection between the deep, spark of originality inside us and our world.

My soul wants to go nightwalking. When I hear the rain clattering on the skylight, or see the trees' shadows dance wildly, I want to be out in it. I know that, on the edge of the village, there is a place where the streetlight ends and the road leads into darkness. The imaginative child inside me sees this as a veil of darkness to walk across, my soul entering another world only available in the shadows.

In this connected, fractured world, the soul faces us with an intensely human challenge. It asks us to live with joy and shadow. At some time in our life, all of us will be immersed in darkness and fear, so it serves us well to learn to walk out into the night – for joy can surprise us even here.

A life of joy and shadow requires us to be unremittingly honest and face the truths of our existence. We do not need to fill up the infinite space of the universe with meaning and intent. It is tempting to try to find sense in the chaos – but ultimately misguided. Life demands engagement and a grounded foundation for our searching.

Living a fulfilled life involves juggling a number of spheres in our life: work, love, nature, beauty, knowledge, meaning. We cannot escape the long shadows cast by our often brutal world, nor wish away or transcend that which darkens our inner and outer lives.

To re-make soul, we will need to return to simple human concerns, to face down those who stand against beauty, depth, life and imagination; to find the courage and creativity to care for the planet that sustains us.

Patrick Harpur tells us that, whilst *"Spirit is expressed in metaphors of ascent, height, light"*, the soul's metaphors are those of *"descent, depth and darkness"*. Soul, he writes, *"is suspicious of purity, knowing that reality is complex and muddy."* [10]

This – with its earthly challenges and human crises – is a time for soul. A time to grow down and be grounded. A time to return the material earth and our everyday connections. A time of uncertainty and for making soul in the darkness as well as in the light.

Part 1 notes and references

1. *Uncivilisation: the Dark Mountain Manifesto* by Dougald Hine and Paul Kingnorth (The Dark Mountain Project, 2009). The Dark Mountain Project is a network of artists and writers finding new responses to a world in crisis. Always provocative, often brilliant, the manifesto, blog and books set out a genuinely different world view. Find them online at: http://dark-mountain.net

2. The term 'Nature Deficit Disorder' was coined by Richard Louv, to describe the growing disconnection of children from nature, and the damage this has done. See *Last Child in the Woods: Saving Our Children from Nature-deficit Disorder* (Atlantic, 2010) and *The Nature Principle: Human Restoration and the End of Nature-Deficit Disorder* (Algonquin Books, 2013) by Richard Louv: http://richardlouv.com

3. M. Scott Peck writes: *"All things are overdetermined. For any single thing of importance there are multiple reasons"* in *The Road Less Travelled: A New Psychology of Love, Traditional Values and Spiritual Growth* (Simon and Schuster, 1978). In his books, Scott Peck integrates psychology and spirituality and suggests that personal growth isn't a deterministic, quick fix.

4. Ken Wilber from his foreword to *Eyes of the Soul: Exploring Inspiration in Art* by Philip Rubinov-Jacobson (2004), at: http://www.kenwilber.com/writings/read_pdf/61

5. The 'acorn theory' comes from *The Souls Code: In Search of Character and Calling* by James Hillman (Bantam Books, 1997). According to Hillman, this theory, *"proposes...that you and I and every single person is born with a defining image...The theory also attributes to this innate image an angelic or daimonic intention, as if it were a spark of consciousness".*

6. Rippling is a beautiful insight in Irvin Yalom's book, *Staring at the Sun: Overcoming the Terror of Death* (Piatkus, 2011). He writes that we live on after our death through the memories of people we have touched in our life. If a function of a religious after-life is to provide comfort in the sight of death, "*rippling*" also eases the pain of "*staring at the sun*".

7. James Hillman's quote is from *The Souls Code* (cited above).

8. *"The Platonic myth of growing down"* writes James Hillman in *The Soul's Code, "says the soul decends in four modes - via. the body, the parents, place and circumstances. These four ways can be instructions for completing the image you brought with you on arrival"*. Growing down, he tells us, is a necessary antidote to *"upward growth"* that has become a *"biographical cliche"*.

9. In *Outliers: The Story of Success* (Penguin, 2009), Malcolm Gladwell sets out how chance and circumstance of birth are as important in predicting success and achievement as being a 'self-made' person with born 'talent'. From this book the popular idea emerged that to become experts we need to practice our craft – or genius – for 10,000 hours.

10 Patrick Harpur in *A Complete Guide to the Soul* (Rider, 2010), writes of our 'double nature' of spirit and soul. He writes: *"Spirit is expressed in metaphors of ascent, height and light. He flies and soars like Peter Pan or Icarus. He longs for transcendence, to rise above the world. Quickly, arrow-straight, he climbs the holy mountain of self-denial and prayer towards Illumination; or the ladders of Reason towards Enlightenment"*. Soul, on the other hand, *"is expressed in metaphors of descent, depth and darkness. She favours the Underworld and the circuitous route. She is not transcendent but immanent, lying hidden within the world"*.

Part 2
Old stories

Remembering

A voice goes back forty years, evokes a fervent song,
flensed of youth, suffused with sad and ancient wisdoms.

The pebbled laughter of a remembered child ripples through the years
as he turns cartwheels on the beach, kicking up arcs of sand that catch
the breeze, gritting the eye of the grown man who watches him, and weeps.

My memory is replete just before sleep. I know that I will dream
of soft and subtle contradictions – yet wake incomplete.

A determinism

In the therapy culture that has come to dominate our social and psychological conversations, most people assume that early-childhood attachment is *the* main determinant of mental health and personality. How did we reach a place where such a specific experience is regarded as the main predictor of adult psychological functioning?

"Mostly", writes Noam Shpancer, *"...because people who show up in psychologists' offices often turn out to have had chaotic childhoods. From this observation, it is but a short, tempting leap to the conclusion that a chaotic childhood causes psychological disturbance. What such a conclusion fails to consider is the fact that those who had chaotic childhoods and ended up untroubled do not show up at psychologists' offices; and they happen to be the majority."* [11]

There has been little consideration given to challenges to attachment theory and the childhood determinism it promotes. Of course, children should be safely kept and loved, but the prevailing view is that troubled children and adults must be all victims of insecure attachment and, moreover, that a great many of us are damaged in this way.

In her two books, *'The Nurture Assumption'* and *'No Two Alike'*, Judith Rich-Harris challenges this myth of early childhood.[12] Our parents don't really *'fuck us up'* she tells us, nor are we blank slates on which are written the stories of our neglectful childhoods.

For years, post-Freudian psychology has been dominated by this old 'nurture' story. It tells us that the unconscious elements of our personality are constructed from parental (most often maternal) relationships. Attachment and nurture are everything in this world of boundaries, transference and projections; with the upshot that our adult lives have now become a hostage to fortune to our healthy (or otherwise) early attachments.

However, Rich-Harris and others have shown that our inheritence, peer group, adult relationships and social cultures are as important as early bonds. The 'nurture assumption' is also a culturally-specific notion, based on relatively recent Western norms of two-parent, nuclear families. In addition, attachment puts nearly all the emphasis on the mother's role, with the result that many women feel drawn back to the home – a blow to hard-fought gender equality based on questionable assumptions.

It may not be inevitable – except in some cases of trauma, abuse and physical damage – that early experience leads to dysfunctional personality adaptation or mental illness. Even then, people can sometimes find surprising and courageous ways of transcending and overcoming early hardships.

This view of childhood determinism does little justice to the full wonder of lifelong, human development. However, we might find another way of living our lives backwards, as James Hillman invites us to do. Here we look back with curiosity to find rich, reflective meaning and hidden stories (*"so that's what that was about!")*, rather than delving around, looking for the past origins of our current unhappiness.

Nurture as incubation

Whilst the old war between nature and nurture still rages (with neuroscience as the new battleground), there may be another way of thinking about nurture that comes from an acknowledgement of our animal nature.

Simply put, when we are parents, our instincts lead us to keep our young safe until they are grown enough to fend for themselves. We are humans, not horses, so children do not stagger to their feet in the moments after they are born. We learn to walk after several precarious months, and remain helpless for years thereafter. Sometime at the back end of brain-addled adolescence, we might just be mature enough to leave the protection of our parents!

The bonds and attachments that keep children, parents and other care-givers together are crucial in maintaining this connective safety. However they may not determine personality in the ways that generations of proud (and guilty) parents have been led to believe.

There are other perspectives emerging. Positive psychology recognises our strengths and virtues – pre-existing elements of human temperament. Archetypal psychologists think in terms of soul and collective imprints in a deeply-embedded, archetypal 'net' of the mind. Even most developmental psychologists now acknowledge that personality development is lifelong, whilst neuroscientists have suggested that the brain's plasticity enables adaptation and growth throughout life.[13]

Integrating these paradigms offers a new way of re-imagining how human personality might emerge and unfold. In relation to this, nurture can be regarded not simply as a developmental process in itself, but as an incubator in which the child's body and innate character is kept 'safe' (or otherwise) and enabled to grow.

There are so many factors and influences on the 'what and how' of an individual's thoughts, emotions and behaviour, that it is pointless looking for direct causes in the past.

So, of course we must keep our children loved and safe, in order to give them the best chance to grow their souls into the future. However we could go far beyond this if we were to build communities and societies that do this for *all* children; and widened our gaze further to re-imagine a world in which they – and their children too – can live safe and soulful lives.

The primacy of emotion

In the late twentieth century, 'emotion' – alongside 'nurture' – became a touchstone of psychology. Many people now regarded the expression of feelings as a true path to human actualisation. The notion of 'emotional intelligence' emerged, and we learned that emotion has its own seat in the brain, and plays a crucial role in mediating the responses of both mind and body to our environment.

However, in the therapy culture that was emerging, nuance was lost, and for many life coaches and counsellors the 'emotional self' has come to be regarded as the true self.

As a result, people began to pore over their childhoods to find clues to their inadequate nurturing or interrupted development. Some became angry with their parents for what had been 'done' to them as children. Others worked to get 'in touch' with their feelings, hoping that this would somehow make them happier.

In personal development and therapy training, this story was played out time and time again. A group would meet and talk – tentatively and carefully at first. Then someone would tell the others how they felt and others would murmur their congratulations and encouragement. Then another member would pipe up to say how they felt – perhaps in relation to something the first person had said. The expression of 'difficult' emotions from childhood, were particularly valued, although there often seemed little real purpose in expressing them, apart from jumping through the hoops of the workshop.

I do not wish this scepticism to be mistaken for a generalisation. Some people suffer psychological wounds in childhood that need to be healed. Those who have suffered abuse or trauma store heightened emotion in their body and mind, experiencing their life as a series of trauma 'triggers'. For them, unwanted emotional arousal is a primary experience and a sign of major distress.

Recent research suggests that the successful treatment of such emotional wounds is not achieved through emotional expression, but through specific body-mind interventions including guided visualisation, EMDR and other work with the cognitive and imaginative mind.[14]

One effect of this 'emotionalisation' of psychology has been to internalise the dangerous realities of the social and ecological world, creating an generalised expectation of psychological victimhood. If we are to seek richer ways of thinking about feelings, we might regard emotion (through empathy) as a way of connecting with our fellow beings in a wider ecology of mind.

We might also see it as a metaphorical gateway to archetypal truth. This deeper story connects with our myths and dreams; inviting us to see emotion as more than merely something to be expressed.

In the old story, we repressed emotions in order to 'forget' negative childhood experiences. Yet, might we also think of our shying from emotion as an instinctive 'flinch' from the terrifying paradoxes in our lives?[15] Perhaps we must learn to *stay with* (rather than express) these feelings, in order to stand at the edge of something vast, unknown and infinitely important.

The happiness fallacy

Would the world be better if we were 'happy'?

This is what we are told, yet it is another erroneous assumption. We cannot be truly happy – despite our self help, therapy, positive thinking and life coaching – because our therapy culture recycles the world's suffering back inside us, telling us that the problem is one of unhappy individuals and their dysfunctional parents.

In truth, we will only be happy if we address what ails us. David Smail writes that our unhappiness – indeed our very sense of 'self' – has social origins, emerging from the limits of our ability to see beyond what he calls our 'power horizon'. "*Consequently*", he writes, "*we do not know how our world has come into being nor how we operate within it; we stumble around blindfold, full of envy, rage and pain.*"[16]

Here's the cultural problem.

In therapeutic psychology, dysfunction is internalised by pathologising the past. In new-age personal development, the emotional 'self' is elevated and 'self actualisation' set as the goal. In cognitive behavioural therapy and life coaching, personal success and wellbeing is to be achieved through positive thinking and self-belief. Meanwhile, an obsession with spirit, torn from its ritualistic foundation in religion, keeps some of us floating precariously above the surface of the earth, never grounded and helpless to change our world.

This mix leaves us increasingly cynical – or else overly idealistic but ultimately despairing – and we become desperate for the short-term fix or peak experience that will make it all better.

Because modern psychological assumptions are directed inwards to the individual self, the deep connections that could guide us towards a better life are often lost. And, searching for meaning, we often project our imaginations outwards onto mythical and idolic constructions, and 'get religion' or one of its new-age counterparts.

The contemporary emphasis on self, success and shallow versions of spirit means that we humans seldom look down towards the earth or out to the horizon. Even when we do look up, we miss the rich, stark wonder of the teeming life that flocks there, and the bright galaxies that shine down. Instead, we seek to give human meaning or magical purpose to what we see – to explain what simply is.

We *are* connected, not by magic, but within physical, material, cultural, social and ecological systems. The authentic, modern soul is one that is in touch with these deep patterns, and does not shy away from the wilderness or the existential realities or life.

The human soul is animal; transformed – essentially and joyfully – by imagination.

The happiness dilemma

People want instant gratification. They want to be happy, and to stay happy. They want to have more stuff. They believe that this will make them happier. Happiness is the goal!

Yet isn't it futile to seek full-time happiness, when the world is in such a mess? Isn't it dangerous to push away suffering, as if it were not a stark fact of our human life? This disconnection between reality, and the fantasy that we should be shiny, happy people, lies behind much of our distress. Anxiety, stress and depression are all conditions emerging from this naïve mismatch between reality and expectation.

The happiness projects claim it is good to seek happiness. At their core, they are all about positive thinking. "*You're not happy unless you think you're happy*", writes Gretchen Rubin.[17] At the disturbing extreme is a modern conjuring trick called the 'law of attraction'. Positive thinking with knobs on, it promises quick fixes and easy money. It is fairy-dust fantasy – exploitative and misleading. If you suffer or don't get what you want, it implies, then this is your fault for not being attuned with the laws of the Universe.[18]

Imagine we do an experiment, and could take a hundred people and make them happy through positive thinking and other cognitive means. A good thing? In the context of a world facing economic and ecological collapse, gross inequality and global abuse of power, I think this would be a really bad thing to do!

Barbara Ehrenreich, regards positive thinking as a dangerous fiction that turns people from life's reality.[19] The human givens include both joy and suffering; together with the recognition that all humans get ill and die, often as a result of our environments and the way other people have treated us. This faces us up to the fact that some people get lucky or unlucky, and that inequalities and abuses of power play a major part in human suffering. Far from positivity being the path to happiness, it is like living with a blindfold.

The problem is that we don't tell stories about the realities of life, but tales of illusion. Those of us who are able, chase certainty and short-term success. We forget the old wisdoms that tell us that our lives are largely governed by chance, commitment and courage. Even then, happiness and success are not guaranteed.

We need to prepare people psychologically for something different. If we were able to face our day-to-day trials in ways that are grounded and realistic, then this would be a start. We might just be better off – not always happier – but engaged, passionate and sometimes joyful.

Happiness cannot be sustained, but joy *can* be experienced, and may be available in each moment of our lives. And joy doesn't depend on buying 'stuff' or finding 'secrets', but on our ability to connect with the world and tell big stories.

The trouble with spirit

One thing that divides thinking people who should be on the same 'side' (that is, taking a stand against ignorance, exploitation and certainty), is the difficult subject of 'spirit'. The integral and enlightenment movements claim to offer clear frameworks for the integration of human wisdom and knowledge, yet seem obsessed with it. Instead of portraying spiritual development as one strand of human experience, it is given a place at the head of the table.

There is a reluctance on the part of materialists (and traditional theologians) to accept what they see as the vague and inexact language of modern spiritual development to explain anything. Faith claims – as it always has – to tell us something universally true based on the ground of belief, and, in its shallowest forms, rejects evidence that doesn't fit.

Deepak Chopra has done as much as anyone to muddy these waters; yet perhaps he has at last recognised there is a problem. In their book, '*War of the Worldviews*', Chopra and physicist Leonard Mlodinow debate the thorny dilemma of science vs. spirit.[20] If this fledgling conversation can lead to a new 'enlightenment' – by which I mean an emergence of clear thinking and engagement that might enable humankind to save itself – then so much the better.

The trouble with the search for spirit is that it can too easily become a personal quest for enlightenment. In this limited worldview, having a 'spiritual life' becomes a prerequisite for engaged living: a hoop we have to jump through before anything else can be considered. Yet, if anything, the human spirit should emerge *from* material engagement. Spirit means nothing unless it is lived!

At its worst, the spiritual quest leads to blind faith and magical thinking that should be banished to history. So it is a tragedy that some proponents of 'new spirituality' see reason as an enemy, sometimes regarding rationalist thought as something to be only reluctantly accommodated.

No wonder we humans have made such a mess of the world! We are born with the gift of reason, yet just at the time we should be recognising blind faith in old stories as naïve representations of our species' childhood, we don it in another garb, scarcely as sophisticated, just a new (age) form of supernatural fancy dress.

In recent times, because of the courage and clarity of rationalists and people of faith alike, humans have had the freedom to use reason to good purpose. To be inquiring and curious about our world and ourselves. To apply the inner spark, an energetic combination of connection, conscience and calling. To evolve our cultural morality and behaviour. To recognise the beauty of our inner wisdom and presence that we might call 'soul'. To be mature and courageous enough to face up to our mortality, to our personal insignificance in the universe – and to mystery.

The Icarus illusion

If Icarus had got his technology right then perhaps he *would* have been able to fly to the sun? Yet, truth be told, the story tells us, he wasn't built to fly. Rib cage, bone density, wing span: the evolutionary tools of being human are insufficient to sustain flight.

With flying, however, we humans still try to turn back the evolutionary clock. We have taken two paths: the technological one of aviation and space flight, and a spiritual one promising another route to the heavens. The idea of escape is embedded deep in both.

"If only", sigh aviators and meditators alike, *"we could escape the strictures of gravity and ground! If only we could transcend the boundaries of our earthly existence – how free we would be!"*

While space travel and spirit may both carry something of the collective imagination, our material reality still remains.

This 'Icarus illusion' reminds us of the evolutionary boundaries of human influence, perception and significance. ALL spiritual (and technological) projects, however sophisticated they claim to be, however much wax and feathers they meld together, are bids for freedom. They offer a promise that we can throw off evolutionary restrictions and do what the birds (or the gods) can do.

The big mistake that Icarus made was to confuse his desire for the higher experience for the material possibility of achieving it! People still do this today when they interpret consciousness in terms of quantum physics, or invent wild, pseudo-scientific theories about the mysteries thrown up by our material universe.

For a scientist, a mystery is something to be intrigued about, something to find out more about. For a guru or pandit, a mystery is something to be entered into. It is an existential balancing act – that's why the uncertain scientist will hedge her bets and go to church, and why the uncertain spiritual teacher will try to recruit science to his cause!

The cultural dimension is that the experience of spirit (or, we might say, the phenomenological experience of transcendence) is bound up by belief. The words we use to describe such an experience will *always* depend on the frame.

This isn't just a way of saying that all spiritual experiences are equally valid (which, in a way, they are); but to point out that – despite millennia of cultural development – we are no nearer spiritual 'truth' than ever we were.

Icarus's basic problem was that he was trying to get somewhere he ultimately could not reach. He made the fatal error of confusing his desires, fantasies and beliefs around flying, with the actual act of flying itself.

We should learn from his mistake.

The moment is now

Latter day, Rennaisance-man, physicist, drummer and philosopher, Richard Feynmann once wrote, "*...if a thing is not a science, it is not necessarily bad. For example, love is not a science. So if something is said not to be a science, it does not mean that there is something wrong with it; it just means that it is not science.*" [21]

Some muddled, yet influential, new-age thinkers use the language of science to explain their own deeply speculative versions of reality. These writers use the term 'evolution' very differently from the way most biologists would accept. This is not necessarily a problem. It is good for science to be challenged over its methodology and assumptions, and to be broadened out into more integral worldviews.

However the problem goes deeper. For integral philosophers like Ken Wilber, 'spirit' transcends and includes other levels of being.[22] It is subtle and mysterious, and essentially unreachable. For thinkers like Daniel Dennett it is the opposite: spirit is a manifestation of outdated superstition. Evolved human consciousness, in their eyes, must necessarily be material – beautiful and poetic perhaps – but essentially explainable.[23]

Ironically, both these worldviews are hierarchal and exclusive, and both claim to represent a more developed, enlightened view than those that came before. Any true integration must enable inclusion, rather than eliciting a new round in the battle of the worldviews.

People have always had experiences of enlightenment and transcendence. Historically this would have been framed within a religious context; now we can draw upon other paradigms.

Nonetheless, all these are still just different lenses to see through. A human experience – transcendent or materialist – is a human experience. It might be explained by science (a god spot in the brain, perhaps), by a traditional religious belief in the afterlife, or through a spiritual meeting of self with universal consciousness in the 'here and now'. Perhaps all we can say is that the explanation is not always relevant to the experience!

One popular 'enlightenment' idea is what Eckhart Tolle calls *"the power of now."*[24] This construct uses the self-help language of new-age psychology, but essentially recognises what many traditions do: that a mindful, meditative state of presence can be profound and powerful. Again science has something to say: the brain chemistry and benefits of meditative states can now also be demonstrated through advances in neuroscience.

In truth, there's little (spiritually) new under the sun. I have my own practice of meditation and experiences of deep connection, but I am sceptical of contemporary spiritual ideas of universal consciousness and transcendence. These seem to me to be speculative and misleading and have little evidence to support them. It seems the ultimate in grandiosity to claim, as some do, that the human mind is instrumental in the evolutionary consciousness of the universe.

Still, states of enlightenment feel wonderful and transcendent. And though they are not science, such experiences – like love – deserve a place in the integral, human experience.

Part 2 notes and references

11. Quotes from *The Myth of Infant Determinism* by Noam Shpancer at *Psychology Today* (2010): http://www.psychologytoday.com/blog/insight-therapy/201009/the-myth-infant-determinism

12 *The Nurture Assumption: Why Children Turn Out the Way They Do* (Bloomsbury, 1999) and *No Two Alike: Human Nature and Human Individuality* (Norton and Co., 2007) by Judith Rich-Harris. These two books provide a counterpoint to the cultural assumptions of childhood determinism that lie behind most social policy in the US, UK and beyond. She also provides a sharp rejoinder to Philip Larkin's poem, *This be the verse* (from his *Collected Poems* (Farrar Straus and Giroux, 2001) and online at: http://www.poetryfoundation.org/poem/178055) which begins:

> *They fuck you up, your mum and dad.*
> *They may not mean to, but they do.*
> *They fill you with the faults they had*
> *And add some extra, just for you.*

Rich Harris writes back:

"Poor old Mum and Dad: publicly accused by their son, the poet, and never given a chance to reply to his charges. They shall have one now, if I may take the liberty of speaking for them:

> *How sharper than a serpent's tooth*
> *To hear your child make such a fuss.*
> *It isn't fair – it's not the truth -*
> *He's fucked up, yes, but not by us". (The Nurture Assumption, p330).*

13. See, for example, *The 21st Century Brain: Explaining, Mending and Manpulating the Mind* by Steven Rose (Vintage, 2006).

14. *Healing without Freud or Prozac Natural Approaches to Curing Stress, Anxiety and Depression* by David Servan-Schreiber (Rodale, 2011) provides evidence of interventions that heal depression and anxiety by harnessing our body and mind's capacity for self-healing.

15. *The Flinch* is a free e-book by Julien Smith (The Domino Project, 2011), that draws on martial arts, parkour and security work to provide a practical psychological wisdom.

16. David Smail has been writing about the social origins of the self for many years. His radical anti-therapy stance challenges us to question many of the assumptions about the origins of psychological distress and what can be done about it. One of his most recent publications, summarising his ideas, is *Power, Responsibility and Freedom* (2010), an online publication available at: http://www.davidsmail.info/intpub.htm

17. From Gretchen Rubin's *Happiness Project* website, online at: http://www.happiness-project.com/happiness_project/2011/11/the-eight-splendid-truths-of-happiness/

18. The 'law of attraction' is a new-age theory, claiming that positive, energy-attuned thinking attracts success, happiness and wealth. It was popularised by Rhonda Byrne's book, *The Secret* (Simon and Schuster, 2006).

19. *Smile or Die: How Positive Thinking Fooled America and the World* by Barbara Ehrenreich (Granta Books, 2010).

20. *War of the Worldviews: Where Science and Spirituality Meet – And Do Not* by Deepak Chopra and Leonard Mlodinow (Three Rivers Press, 2012).

21. Richard Feynmann from *Six Easy Pieces: Essentials of Physics Explained by Its Most Brilliant Teacher* (California Institute of Technology, 1963).

22. Ken Wilber's integral model claims to be the most complete 'theory of everything'. The idea that certain spiritual states equate to the highest modes of human development is controversial, and not shared by all integral theorists. A good introduction to integral theory can be found on the Integral Life website: https://integrallife.com

23. Daniel Dennett is popularly regarded as a leading proponent of the 'new atheism', but is a more subtle philosopher, steering a course between the immortal soul of religion, and the moral wasteland of scientific determinism. In his book, *Freedom Evolves* (Penguin, 2003), he makes the argument for free-will and morality that is biological rather than spiritual in essence.

24. *The Power of Now: A Guide to Spiritual Enlightenment* by Eckarte Tolle (Hodder, 2001).

Part 3
The wild psyche

Turning

I turn to the clouds over the hills and feel layers of colour seep into me.
There is deep purple at the base and a hundred words for grey
climbing to the silver trails vapouring at the tips of majestic columns.

I turn to the raptors as they spin and hunt, high in the silver.
Held there by my tired gaze, they soar away. I want to emulate
their indifference, but my pale imitation is washed out by the wind.

I turn to the hills, and I want to ground myself:
burying deep into the bluestone, dithering rough in the moorland,
nesting in the clefts and furrows of the cool highland summer.
Now I must speak again, for the wild pathways have been prepared.

Giving the *id* its head

In one old story, Sigmund Freud wrote: *"From the very first we have said that human beings fall ill of a conflict between the claims of instinctual life and the resistance that arises within them against it."* [25]

Freud's *id* (or 'it') was always the instinctual, animal side of us, the hidden drive that must emerge into the light and be dissipated by our rational minds.

Perhaps this old story has it wrong? Maybe the importance of the *id* is not in its mediation by the super-ego in a battle of control for our self, but the potential it holds for freedom and release? Wars, after all, are not waged by uncontrolled *ids*, but by grandiose egos who present their programme as all that matters – justifying their actions with judgemental, super-hero values. These cultural values are dangerous and contradictory weapons. Where would we be – ask our super-ego leaders and cultural arbiters – without morality? Anarchy and madness would prevail!

Anarchy is not a creed that has led to extermination and state oppression, nor one held by those who have degraded our planet so gravely in the name of civilisation. The civilised amongst us always claim morality and sanity (usually 'God' too) for their side, and proclaim themselves the enemies of madness.

We can note here that state mental health systems have often been potent weapons against dissent and difference. State-registered sanity has not been always a straightforward force for good, and individual psychology does not equate with social culture unless it is structured that way, and we have been mostly blind to this construction.

Here's a thought. If left to its own devices, perhaps the *id* might simply act out its desires? Some people might get hurt – but millions are hurt and killed now by the actions of 'rational' minds. And many more have been harmed, as the shadows of our civilisation are perpetually projected out onto 'them' – enemies to be defended against, whose lives are ultimately dispensable as the end of protecting 'us' justifies the means.

Little *ids* flying around would not be comfortable, but could make for a more exciting, soulful way to live our lives. Meaning often emerges most clearly in the imaginative enactment of desire, not through its concealment and repression! Love is easier and more passionate without the strangling of super-ego morality. And through the lens of an *id*-led culture, commerce, mass entertainment and politics would be recognised as mechanisms of control and products of a poverty of mind. Life would be revealed as life.

So, let them out to play and our *ids* might reveal themselves as wonderful, archetypal, alchemical elements that can turn cultures into communities. We might find that we acquire that magical, touchstone quality which comes when people act as if they have no place in history.

The call of the wild

Some people are framing new thinking about our wild minds. They champion the wisdom of indiginous peoples and question the notion of progress in our civilisation. Philosophers such as Joanna Macy and David Abram, show how our psychological and physical separation from the wild has been profoundly and progressively damaging, and tell us that a renewed connection is needed.[26, 27]

Meanwhile, eco-psychologists like Nick Totton suggest that a return to the wild places in the psyche is a necessary response to the failure of our increasingly unimaginative civilisation and therapy culture.[28]

These writers are claiming back the wild for psychology; building a renewed understanding of the interdependent and imaginative qualities of our human world. In this context, 'going wild' means having the psychological courage and vision to go beyond culturally constructed walls. Such practitioners see it as essential to begin to embrace imaginative wildness in a necessary therapy of activism.

Others, however, seem determined to keep civilised norms intact; to keep psychotherapy within deterministic, clinical and state sanctioned boundaries and enclosures.[29] The adoption by much of the profession of the term 'clinician' reveals how deeply the practices of therapy have become embedded within medical parameters and are subject to the myths of diagnosis and the 'rigours' of evidence-based practice.

Whilst a medical view of mental anguish cannot be discarded (all approaches carry *some* truth), the institutionalisation of helping holds the risk that the fullness of our human nature will never be fulfilled.

We live in a culture that cannot tolerate wildness and continues to regard psychological distress as emerging from *inside* the client – a result of genetics or domestic history carried from their families.

In this frame, therapists are not activists, but careful, tentative practitioners offering to rebuild some semblance of domestic bliss. For them, the call of the wild seems a chaotic howl. Their task is to help troubled people function – those who did not develop proper childhood attachments and boundaries – and develop civilised ways of adult functioning and relating.

Reducing suffering is a good thing to do, but many psychologists do not grasp that much human sadness and dysfunction is caused by wider social and ecological disconnections – and so cannot be sustainably turned around by therapy.[30] For such clinicians, 'wildness' (which acknowledges savage pain) challenges the premise of what they do, and entertaining such an approach goes beyond the pale.

Psychological wildness can, of course, seem terrifying for people who (as most therapists have done) spend years learning to be happy within nurturing, civilised walls! Sadly, this fear can lead to blind projections of the world's chaos into their clients' madness. In short, these practitioners swallow the old stories whole.

This being so, we might argue that having given up the opportunity to inhabit the shamanic spaces at the edge of the wild, therapists have lost the right to be seen as soul-makers. Yet, who will reveal soul if psychologists and therapists will not?

Our multiple voices

In a new psychology of wildness, we have an opportunity to recognise that when our myriad voices speak, they articulate a wider humanity. This is an intuitive, ancient wisdom, yet psychology has often regarded voices from inside us as symptoms of pathology or, at best, hidden, dream-like figures to be metaphorically unveiled. When they emerge, these are to be integrated into an authentic 'self' we can call our own.

This focus on a singular self is like spending a lifetime in a forest exploring a single tree – ignoring the rich and diverse ecosystem all around. Whilst we can never fully know ourselves (so sticking to the 'one tree' version of self-hood might seem more manageable), so much is missed in this limited exploration, for the forest – like each multi-faceted person – grows and changes with time and circumstance.

Our psychology has civilised us into accepting the illusion of a 'self'. In our everyday lives, it suits us to experience a sense of 'I'; yet if we pause for a moment, we become be aware of so much more than this. Being open, even in an instant, I can become aware of the full potential of my experience; a sense of 'my-self' carrying different sub-personalities, each emerging in subtle and not-so-subtle ways. This can feel disconcerting – even fragmenting. We would be more comfortable by sticking with the ego – the 'me' that does the job of 'I' so very well.

Bruce Hood beautifully describes the process of the ego waking each morning: "*As the slumber recedes into the night, we awake to become who we are. The morning haze of dreams and oblivion lifts as recognition and recall bubble up the content of our memories into our consciousness. For the briefest of moments we are not sure where we are and then suddenly 'I', the one who is aware, awakens."* [31]

This 'ego' is an illusion. We might more usefully think of the self as a dynamic interplay of our inherited disposition with our interactions with the external world. In a short and insightful paper, self psychologist, Ernest Wolf wrote, *"I think of the self not as a structure, not as particular area of the mind but as an organization of the memory traces of a certain type and kind of experiences."* [32]

In Integral Psychology, the self is recognised as consisting of different sub-personalities. All have awareness, but none feel intrinsically like an 'I'. The nearest we get to this is what Wilber calls the 'proximate self': *"some sort of observing self (an inner subject or watcher)"* – keeping an eye on the other bits of us.[33]

What we experience as self or consciousness fluctuates from moment to moment. From a body awareness of being warm, to a cognitive awareness of sorting out a problem. From a deep awareness of something bubbling up from within, to a subtle awareness of our connection with the world. From an emotional connection with an old memory, to an archetypal awareness of a shadow that darkens our life momentarily. From a memory of a line of poetry, to the joy of connecting with a loved one. And so on.

In the final analysis we are not singular beings at all. So we might do as well to follow *all* the voices that approximate to 'I' 'me' and 'us'; to explore as much of the forest as we are able in our lifetimes.

Where in the world?

Through the integration of deep and simple wisdoms, it may be possible for therapy to be reconstructed as a powerful space in which to have the conversations our imaginations deserve. This reframing of our psychological architecture would enable the helping conversation to evolve into a soulful, social and ecological meeting in which healing, solace, therapy, guidance and counsel is offered and received.

Re-constructing psychotherapy as deep and simple helping will bring our experiences of body and soul, family and culture, world and wilderness into the conversation. It will helps us shift our relationship to each other, to the earth and the lifeforms that share it with us. This process has the potential to take what is called therapy beyond self, self-help and clinical interventions, and offering the possibility of rich metaphorical explorations of our being in the world. It is precisely at this juncture that a political dimension to these manifestos is required.

In an interview, the psychoanalyst and writer, Adam Phillips said: "*I think that psychoanalysis is a symptom of despair about political life, and I think people should go via psychoanalysis back to political social life, not take refuge in it. It seems to me a very interesting cultural moment when people begin to feel they need to speak to someone who's not a religious person, nor a member of the family. I would prefer a world in which people spoke to their friends or family. I hope that psychoanalysis will help people use the resources in their social group better*". [34]

If psychotherapy has a cultural task in our society, it is to bring the psychological conversation out of the secret gardens of professional language and assumptions about the self, and back into the real world.

In writing this I recall a conversation with an old friend. Dave Hicks has a quiet wisdom, and his twinkle-eyed gentleness belies a sharp, radical intelligence. In his office in Bath we talked of therapy and the ways we humans strive for happiness in a fractured world.

Dave is respectful of psychological insight, yet asks big questions of those of us who strive to make people happy and sane in an unhappy and insane world: *"where is the global dimension, where is justice, where is the future – where is the world in all this?"* [35]

And hearing him, we can also ask: "*Where is the world? Where is the soul? Where are the deep conversations and stories we need? And how on earth can therapy help people make meaning, when our minds and lives (like our cities and communications) have become overcrowded, confused and bombarded?*".

If psychotherapy is to have a role in helping people with the problems and direction of their lives, then it must be more about these broader questions, and less about diagnosis and short-term patching up. In short, if therapy is not obsessed so narrowly with people getting 'better', then it holds the potential for something more.

Only then might *"the good words of a conversation"* – as poet David Whyte puts it – become a meeting place where lives can be changed, and from where the world can be changed in its turn.[36]

Will you step through?

"Above the door, we see the terrible figure,
fierce eyes demanding, 'Will you step through?'"
(David Whyte, 2007)[37]

A fearsome shadow dares us to cross a threshold into darkness. Here we face our greatest fears and the realisation of our eventual death. There is a simple choice: to enter or refuse – and why would we step across if we wish a joyful life? Why not simply refuse the shadow's call, close the door and banish the darkness?

The simple answer is that knowing ourselves fully is joyful. Step across, and we will, in David Whyte's poignant words, be *"wedded to our essence"*. Facing the un-faceable, stepping into the dark places in our soul, allowing ourselves (despite ourselves) to go where we fear most, gives us a deep sense of knowledge, liberation and potential. And if we do decide to turn away, the shadow lives to fight again, emerging more fiercely the next time around.

Often we face our life's challenges on the shadow's threshold. There always seems to be a fierce and terrible figure at this place. Though we have nowhere else we can go, we stand frozen and fearful. At this edge, the only appropriate emotion is fear, the only impulse is to escape, the only intuition is of death. Yet we must summon our greatest courage and step right through the shadow's chilling veil.

On the other side we may sit and rest – exhilarated and chastened. We may realise that our own discarded shadow self always held the key to our freedom.

Now, newly born and freshly made, we see that we are as beautiful and joyful as the day.

Facing our shadow is part of knowing all the parts of our self – warts and all. And to look in a mirror – free of the holdings, avoidances, pushing-asides and projections that limit our lives and relationships – is to be joyful. Facing the shadow allows us to love ourself; not boastfully, but with self-compassion and realism. There is relief too at not having to continue the pretence that we are without sin, flaw, wound and suffering.

The playful Jungian analyst Harry Wilmer wrote:
"All the demonic things by which human beings betray their inhumanity to other beings is shadow.
Shadow is unconscious, therefore, we encounter our shadow in other people, things and places where we project it." [38]

He recognised that facing shadow is a prerequisite to soul-making. This is as true in the outer social world as it is in the inner world of imagination, memory and archetype. Being an activist and challenging the world's shadows (whilst taking responsibility for our part in their creation and continuation) is a serious business. When shadows gets loose, they get up to terrible things.

Nevertheless, if we are careful, we may find a fundamental intuition. This tells us that the light of hope dispels shadow, and that carrying hope for the world is as necessary a piece of work as facing our own individual shadow and healing our self.

A faery child

Deep in the heart of a wood wanders a lone child. She is fascinated, absorbed in the dappled magic of the place, eager to explore, keenly aware of birdsong, acutely attuned to the subtle variations of her world. From time to time she stops, timelessly suspended in an eternal now of imagination. Aware of the god in each small thing and of the veil she has crossed. Aware of the rustling, whispered, wild grace of this deep and endless place that is her birthright.

She is a *faery* child – fey – at once serious and joyful. At this early stage in life, her morality is unfixed, ethics grounded purely in consequence. She knows instinctively that harm is inevitable, and that to cause it is wrong. Beyond this, there are few boundaries; though she will learn these in time and, in doing so, may lose sight of herself.

In our nature, as children, we all have our own version of the *faery*. This is an archetype seldom touched upon; it is smaller and less grandiose than the Mother, Warrior, Mage or *Puer Aeternis.*[39] She is grounded in the everyday, not the eternal. Her concerns are secular rather than spiritual, phenomenological rather than transcendent, poetic rather than operatic. Her soul is not purposeful Gaia, yet she carries within her the incidental, accidental, miraculous specks of life that pepper our world.

She is tentative, naïve, curious and sure of her destiny – as far as her intuitive wisdom takes her. She is free and joyful, yet vulnerable to a fear of dark places and to pain when she is hurt. At these times, the fey child – open, honest and true – may need the calm hand of a grown-up who understands. This parental figure will give comfort and love, then allow the child to slip once more across the veil.

As we grow, the *faery* in each of us is diminished and turned from. This speck of magic inside that knows beauty and freedom can fade. Too many adults have their *faery* die inside, through the disbelief of their family, culture and peer group, or caged by the subtle exhortations of others. Others lose innocence in more brutal ways.

Sometimes it is our parents who fear the wild *magyck* of the child's spirit. Or, in order to fit in, the child herself decides. With stark determination, the perilous sprite is put aside or hidden, to become in time the subject of disbelief.

For some bright souls, the spirit of their connection with the world's magic is too strong. A deep and lifelong struggle ensues between the grey socialisations of human families and cultures and the spark of dancing light that gives them hope that one day they will be able to return to themselves.

In this story of lost childhood, the key archetype is not the Little Prince or Peter Pan (the eternal boy with his sure and grandiose crowing), but Tinkerbell, whose life depends on the belief of those around her.[40]

And if we don't clap our hands, she fades and is lost.

Hooray for them!

I recently became a grandfather and so, after a twenty-odd year gap, I have been put in touch again with the awesome energy, wisdom and love encapulated in the intimate presence of a young child.

This little soul has taken me apart; I have fallen in love with her and want to champion an understanding of her character and calling that will ease a joyful, carefree way for her unique little self (and all those others born around her), in what has become a superficial, judgemental, often cruel and soulless world.

Children and adolescents are misunderstood and often mistreated. Their wishes, desires and fantasies are derided and put aside. Their rich potential is reduced, at such a young age, to the factory outputs of 'comparitive achievement' and 'developmental milestones', when what is so wonderful about them is that they just want to *be.*

Childhood has been pinned down and made literal. *Faeries* are no longer wild creatures of imagination living at the edges of a child's world (in the fields and edges of the garden), but cartoon characters (fairies) with American accents and merchandising deals.

In the old world, the *faery* was the child, flying through familiar landscapes – and the monster too, tramping through the woods, fierce, small and wonderful. This child only needs an adult to fend off the fiercer animals (a cat, in my two-year-old granddaughter Freya's case!), and to comfort her when she's hurt herself, so she can tramp off again into the wild when she's feeling better.

However, some adults still champion children. Hooray for them!

I love the way, in particular, that Jay Griffiths champions children's sly, sensual sparks of imagination and their desire to burrow into the earth and shut out the adult world.[41] She, unlike our policy makers, politicans and cultural arbiters, is not afraid of children's wildness, nor does she give a hoot about whether they are going to be competitive in a global market when they do their Key Stage 1 Maths assessments.

What she (and I) care about is that our children can grow up to be engaged and soulful adults, in a world that is more sanely and sustainably run than it is now.

We want, in the meantime, for Freya and her generation of little ragamuffins, scarecrows and *faery* children to be able to explore their world widely, live out their natures, and grow up (but not too soon!) into flourishing trees from the small seeds of their potential and soul they have carried since birth.

A grown up kind of happiness

"Happiness is the result of inner maturity. It depends on us alone and requires patient work carried out from day to day".
(Matthieu Ricard, 2003)[42]

Matthieu Ricard reminds us that achieving happiness is a lifelong, renewable process rather than a permanent state. It is a way through to something intrinsic, not simply a cognitive response to circumstance.

For the fortunate child, childhood can be a glorious place. For this child, her very immaturity leads to happiness: the ways she follows her needs and desires so closely, and finds delight in simple, stupid things. Happiness is possible for this child because there is no requirement for her to be anything but immature. But if immaturity lingers, it confuses her and looming adulthood can begin to seem an unsettling journey into the unknown.

Maybe it is not surprising that many of us find it difficult to be a grown-up. Perhaps we cannot be wholly blamed for our holding on to lingering immaturities. Growing up (and growing down) are confusing, and there are few rituals of initiation remaining that help us pass through.

On the one hand, we are urged to listen to our 'inner child'. On the other, we must take our responsibilities seriously. The carrot of quick-fix success is dangled before us, as numerous 20- and 30-something celebrities publish their autobiographies – as if they have discovered a secret the rest of us missed. TV screens are filled daily with shiny, happy people, satiating themselves with food, sex, fame and consumption – or their own drug of choice.

Here's the thing: there can be no quick fix, and there is no secret. Wisdom comes with experience. It tells us that there is no guarantee of lifelong happiness. The best we can hope for is to negotiate our path with maturity, openness and presence, and when we live like this, we notice there are numerous moments of joy waiting for us.

Sometimes it is the lingering presence of the immature, needy, childish self that can be an obstacle. When I am inwardly immature, I find it difficult to touch joy. Somehow, a sullen blanket of bruised entitlement and *"it's not fair"* can cover my world and conceal its potential. I feel put in my place, as a child might, and familiar, habitual insecurities can move me from happiness.

Unfaced, these feelings could turn into the selfish habits of narcissism, and the shallow charms and selfish manipulations of the child-mind masquerading – with grandiose authority – as an adult. It's fine to hold onto our playfulness, spontaneity and attachments – but not to mistake childish buffoonery, the safety of habit and a desire for reassurance for grown-up, grounded happiness.

The spirit of a connection

As we become grown, our disconnection from ourselves can become deeply painful. Often, it is those who come to talk in therapy who seem most aware of this pain. It is as if these people grieve for something we have all lost that is deeply important to the human soul. The lost archetype of childhood is in this loss. It is remembered by us all, but most of all by the *faery* children who are most connected with magic in the world.

Happiness is contradictory. Some of the most unhappy people also carry an enormous capacity for sensitivity, joy and creativity. They seem willing to occupy the psychological 'borderlands' in ways others are not.[43] Whilst this might lead them to pain and sorrow as much as to joy, they have a wonderful capacity to reveal beauty.

They know that the world they are born into is not the one they were born for. They do not fit the socialised human world; are more comfortable walking barefoot, in touch with the earth and its rhythms, hills, oceans, forests, plains and creatures.

It requires honesty and a sense of great resilience to live with this contradiction. Such people often live courageous lives that are profound and fulfilled. They ask big questions and do not fear despair as the rest of us do. For them, after all, it is a familiar companion.

These are the children who are always stirring. They rebel against or refuse the socialised norms of economic and political cynicism and greed. They creep across the veil between this world and the imagined, putting aside safety for the adventure of spirit.

These are the wise, childish voices of our conscience. They carry the world's tragedy and sadness, but also its potential for simple joy.

Perhaps these were the serious children, whose inner maturity was set from the start? Emotionally and spiritually precocious, they were always tuned into the pain of the world, sometimes too much so for their own good. Nonetheless, their 'inner children' can teach us something important about growing with joy. We should honour them as the soul-guides of our age. If we listen to them carefully, they can teach us lessons, not of shallow happiness, but of life.

And they promise something else: a hint of discovering something like our true selves – an authentic spirit, free of the constraints and denials we construct around our lives as we grow.

And above all: imagination.

Interlude: Drawn back

It can be a random thing that triggers it. A touch of familiar scent or wind on my face in a particular place or time of day, or a brush with beauty or pain. It can be a realisation of happiness – then a fear of losing what is precious. There might be a memory, a thought or tinctured evocation of something past that carries emotion.

Such visitations are touched with poignancy. I am rarely nostalgic for what was real, more for what I did not have back then. In a way, this feeling of loss is irrational. It seems more a sense of losing something I wished I'd had, rather than something that is actual or absent.

Yet it is so real.

In moments like these I wonder if it is only me? Perhaps, over time, I have become hard-wired (that hateful, mechanical, little phrase) to experience the world like this. Or is there something in the human condition that evokes a twisted sense of nostalgia in us all?

I am not sure how much it matters which is true, or whether both can co-exist simultaneously. There is a temptation here to draw back into theory and the twentieth century debates: nature vs. nurture; evolution vs. blank slate; developing personality vs. original soul.

There is another false divide between science and poetry. The first searches for truth that can be proven; the second for words to prove truth. I want to resist the temptation to get into this debate; to stay with the experience and become aware of what is evoked.

I stay with this question: *"am I alone or is this something shared?"*.

The boy. His search for love. Loss. Experience only imagined. Dreams of richly-coloured, hinted-at meaning. Beaches now, beaches then. What it could mean to be a poet or a scientist (or whatever else I was born to be!). The acorn encapsulates all this – yet these are still only partial and selective stories.

"Life has five plots:
"rise to fame, fall to grace,
gain love, lose it
and death", writes Peter Finch.[44]

I might add a sixth: the yearning for all these. In this sixth plot lies a clue to what draws us back to re-explore ancient grounds. The archaeology of the soul has yearning at its heart.

I come back full circle: *"is this yearning mine or is it universal?"*.

See how the question seems to want to matter – to demand attention.

Part 3 notes and references

25. Sigmund Freud, in *New Introductory Lectures on Psycho-analysis, Lecture XXXI The Dissection of the Psychical Personality* (1933) in *The Standard Edition of the Complete Psychological Works of Sigmund Freud.* The lecture is online at: www.yorku.ca/dcarveth/Freud%20NIL%20L33%20Dissection.pdf

26. *World as Lover, World as Self: A Guide to Living Fully in Turbulent Times* (Parallex Press, 2007) and *Coming Back to Life: Practices to Reconnect Our Lives, Our World* (New Society Publishers, 1998)by Joanna Macy. Find out more at: http://joannamacy.net and http://workthatreconnects.org.

27. *The Spell of the Sensuous: Perception and Language in a More-Than-Human World* (1997) and *Becoming Animal: An Earthly Cosmology* (2011) by David Abram (Vintage Books). His website is: http://wildethics.org

28. *Wild Therapy: Undomesticating Inner and Outer Worlds* by Nick Totton, (PCCS Books, 2011).

29. Denis Postle claims that the psychological professions have 'enclosed' and professionalised what he refers to as the Psy-commons: *"The psyCommons is a name for the universe of rapport – of relationship between people – through which we navigate daily life"*: from *Therapy Today* (Volume 24, Issue 3, April 2013). There's more on his website: https://wildernessweb.org

30. Although the consensus amongst therapists (and more widely in our culture) is that counselling 'works', this isn't the view of some. David Smail has argued that therapy ignores the social sources of distress, and a recent book by Paul Maloney –*The Therapy Industry: The Irresistible Rise of the Talking Cure, and Why It Doesn't Work* (Pluto Press, 2013) – continues the theme, providing a cogent challenge to the assumptions of our therapy culture.

31. *The Self Illusion: Why There is No 'You' Inside Your Head* by Bruce Hood (Constable, 2012).

32. *Mutative Moments in the Psychoanalytical Experience* by Ernst Wolf, (1999) online at: www.selfpsychology.com/papers/wolf_1999.htm

33. *Integral Psychology – Consciousness, Spirit, Psychology, Therapy* by Ken Wilber (Shambhala Publications, 2011).

34. Interview with Adam Phillips in *Counselling and Psychotherapy Journal* (CPJ), (April 2005).

35. David Hicks' books include: *A Climate Change Companion* (CreateSpace, 2017) & *Educating for Hope in Troubled Times* (Trentham Books, 2014).

36. Quote from poem, *Loaves and Fishes,* by David Whyte, *The House of Belonging* (Many Rivers Press, 1996) and online at www.davidwhyte.com/english-poetry#Loaves

37. Quote from poem, *The Faces at Braga,* by David Whyte, *Where Many Rivers Meet* (Many Rivers Press, 2007).

38. *Practical Jung: Nuts and Bolts of Jungian Psychotherapy* by Harry Wilmer (Chiron Publications, 1987).

39. The *puer aeternis* archetype is also known as the Peter Pan syndrome or eternal boy. A key book is *The Problem of the Puer Aeternus* by Marie-Louise Von Franz (Inner City Books, 2000), but this Wikipedia entry gives a good basic introduction: https://en.wikipedia.org/wiki/Puer_aeternus

40. *Peter Pan and Wendy* by J. M. Barrie (Hodder and Stoughton, 1911)

41. *Kith: The Riddle of the Childscape* by Jay Griffiths (Hamish Hamilton, 2013)

42. Mattieu Ricard quoted in *Buddhist Offerings, 365 Days* (Thames and Hudson, 2003).

43. *Living in the Borderland: The Evolution of Consciousness and the Challenge of Healing Trauma* by Jerome S. Bernstein (Routledge, 2005). Bernstein identifies 'borderland' personality traits. These include connection to nature and the world, as well as feelings of social isolation and a sense of the sacred in experience. The 'borderland' personality is at the heart of the *faery* child archetype. Find more information at: www.livingintheborderland.com

Interlude: Drawn back

44. Quote from poem, *Llywelyn Goch ap Meurig Hen at Speed,* by Peter Finch (*Poetry Review,* Volume 93, No 2, Summer 2003).

Part 4
Constellations

String theory

Morning: I am aware of a million layers curled up in the sky
and watch strings of geese unravel in a diffuse, blue scattering.

Driving past Dyffryn Ceidrych, yearning drags me towards the ancient mound.
As the kites circle, I rise up through the mist from below, down with the light,

down through the earth – where the rhizomorph world is all connected –
up through the sky where light flows from butterfly wings and

strings of migration vibrate in us like pangs of memory. My song is sung
sidelong into the world as I kneel and scrabble in the loaming earth

in search of the elusive particle, like panning for gold. There is more chance
of finding it here than in some airborne string theory. Each layer of the sky

has its own nature, gravity existing for one brane within the bulk.
A whisper becomes a ferocious destiny; here the wind becomes a feather.

Imagination is dangerous

We might say that joy is only truly possible when our imagination is fully alive. Conversely, joylessness lies in the failure of imagination. To be joyful is to be courageously imaginative, to have a vision that transcends the familiar. This touches upon unsuspected, beautiful places where nothing is predictable or ordinary. Here the chaotic and surreal can be vibrant and unrestrained within us.

Yet imagination is dangerous. Our civilisation is preoccupied with the maintainance of sanity and order. We fear disorder so profoundly that we nip it in the bud wherever we see it. This is never so true as in childhood, where the anarchic potential of imagination is most stark: *"culture, the child's upbringing as it is called, is about tempering the madness of fantasy"*, wrote Adam Phillips.[45]

We still search for that mad, joyous imagination. Yet, because we fear madness so much, our imagination fails us and we push away the child once more. And if we cannot imagine something different, we end with the crumbling same. Successful, authentic organisations value imagination and creativity above all else. Progressive cultural and political systems need imagination at their heart, or else they become stagnant and self-serving.

The great imagineer, Ben Okri, asks us to consider having, *"a sense of beauty about the shape of our lives"*. In doing so, he champions the aesthetic sense that writers bring to their practice of storytelling. They ask us to look into the glass and see beyond the familiar face we present to the world, with its predictability of habit. *"The best life"*, he tells us, *"and the life we would really want to live, is on the other side of the mirror."* [46]

Imagination brings the joy of self-discovery. Despite the potential for pain in the self-awareness that comes from looking into the mirror, we are most joyful when imagination is touched, and when the creative image or word is allowed to spontaneously emerge.

I, like millions of others, have been conditioned to sanity, common sense and normality. Sometimes the challenges of getting and keeping work, and being careful and responsible, take over. At these times I do not wish to be seen as mad, bad or flawed – just to be heard, understood and accepted.

Nonetheless, my best times are when I am tapping into the deepest of wells inside myself. Then I am filled to the brim with colourful, vibrant images, ideas, words and possibilities. Here, emotion and thought can be chaotic and disintegrated; my vision is surreal and nonsensical. Here I can be childlike, playful and carefree.

It is also at these times that I have the potential to reach out and touch others – to offer them a hint of this joy. Even if they too are averse to madness, perhaps a piece of my infectious imagination will rub off and make a difference. And conversely, when the imaginations of people I am with are firing on all cylinders – that is to say, when their own imaginative visions and poetic images emerge – at these times I too am inspired.

The invisible 'I'

So what lies on the other side of the mirror?

Imagination, surely, but something else too. Human beings always have a notion of what lies within – a sense of something other than the conscious, concrete outer-life that is measurable and touched.

Sometimes we externalise this intuition, and call it God. Or we may sense a connection – a touch of magic that has no rules – and in dreams glimpse its unfamiliar forms. It emerges in both expected and unexpected places: in art and writing, in habits and behaviour, in the stories we are told, and in our sense of a 'self' that seems to lie both inside and outside our physical being.

We also call this thing the 'unconscious', yet it carries more than a repressed set of historical experiences. It can sometimes seem like a universe in itself; infinitely recreating; constantly reworking the material of memory, experience, archetype and calling; recycling all this with the dynamic energy and potential we call 'soul'.

It is not possible to locate a notion of 'I' anywhere in particular, and so we only have an approximation of a self we have learned to be. We develop metaphors of self through dreams, memory and inner experience and these also contribute to a sense of 'me'. Such experiences can become energetic – having pain, fear or joy associated with them; in other words, they attract our psychological attention.

This can lead to habits of avoidance or compulsion, together with a false and partial sense of identity.

Despite this, I can still have a congruent sense of my self. There will be moments in which I feel clouded and indistinct, fragmented or torn. At other times I feel lucent and clear, and in these moments of clarity, the inner 'I', outer 'me' and 'we' feel in harmony.

At these times my whole being – body, mind, soul and ecological self – comes together and my dreams, physical sensations, conversations and energies seem aligned. There is a numinous, joyful quality in this integration of which I may not normally be aware.

This invisible 'I' is mostly hidden from view, yet glimmers emerge and I get a hint of something more – a subtle body sensation perhaps, or a gesture that gives a clue to the emotional state lying behind my projected self. There is such joy in catching phosphorescent glimpses of someone (myself) only partly known. And frustration too, for a passing experience of wholeness only leaves me wanting more.

The sustained task, then, is one of exploration. A life spent in touch with (though not lost in) my inner-life, whilst constantly grounded and engaged with the outer-world, is a rich and joyful one. It is an exploration of a constantly unfolding landscape. It provides an evolving awareness of what it feels like to be 'me' in a real and authentic way, and of the forces and energies that influence us.

And where else might we find this joy? Most of all, it is manifested in a person who has a luminous quality in the eyes of those they meet.

Constellations

For some theorists, the invisible 'I' emerges from relationships and attachments in early life. For others, it is determined by the evolution of behaviour and the biochemistry of neural-pathways. For some it is socially constructed, whilst others regards our construction of reality as a philosophical – even spiritual – question.

None of these can fully explain the invisible 'I'.

A cartographer can map the road and features of the landscape – even something of its history. What he cannot do is tell me why, as I see a cloud pass over a hill, I stop the car and watch its shadow darken the ground. He cannot explain how this fleeting moment evokes such a strong complex of emotion and memory. The specific impulse, experience and motivation cannot be explained.

The route can be mapped, an engineer can explain the mechanism of the vehicle that carries me. Inside the car, however, the decisions I make, the songs I play, who is with me, how I feel and how all this connects – what mapmaker, engineer or scientist can know this?

It seems we are traversing the universe of the self on foot. We have hardly started our journey of exploration, let alone reached the moon and stars.

So what can we know? That we are all born with a seed of our self. That each of us has a social history: a set of experiences that we habitually set out in linear fashion, stretching back to birth, providing a join-the-dots picture which becomes an approximation of self.

It is only an outline, because this partial history is made up of an unconscious selection of points of experience. Certain energised (or idealised) memories from the past are 'selected' to construct this story. This story tells us – and those significant others in our world – who I may have been or have not been.

However, whilst these experiences *are* part of our history, we also discard many others. This happens, without us noticing, at the subtle behest of others and through the injunctions of society and culture. We might construct this line of lights in order to avoid experiencing the darkness of our own cold shadows. The result is that we project only one habitual story (and with it, one habitual self) in our interactions with the world.

The wider story can be seen by others, however, and with attention, we can begin to read it ourselves in our dreams, creativity and imagination. It will then start to emerge in the truest ways we express ourselves.

This is a difficult task, but we owe it to ourselves to have knowledge of this inner universe: this constellation of experiences and influences that make us who we are. In touching this deep, fragmented, yet authentic self, we can unveil the wider complexity of the invisible 'I', and begin to tap into the rich veins of gold that lie deep within each of us.

The myth and the archetype

"The lesson of mythology may be...to reconnect what has been scattered. To gather the random notes into a total harmony, chord or refrain".
(Drew Kampion, 2007)[47]

Mythology echoes stories hidden in each one of us and embedded deep within our cultures. In our imaginations, and the collective mind of humanity, lies the joyful potential for all our meetings.

When we realise how everything connects, our defences fall away. No difference can justify any form of manufactured separateness when we understand our shared nature. No actions that damage our world can be justified when we remind ourselves of the deep evolutionary connection we have with our fellow lifeforms and with the earth.

The equality of humanity is a moral and evolutionary truth. Scientists have tracked the genetic origins of humankind to a few families making their way out of Africa, and this perilous journey populated the whole planet within tens of thousands of years. The connections are firmly made, and require no gods, except, perhaps, as powerful archetypes in themselves.

This connectedness doesn't stop with genetic lines. The reawakened awareness of our universal, collective, cultural and imaginative inheritance was Carl Jung's greatest gift to us.

For some, the journey to such a joyful and liberating realisation is a spiritual one. Yet I believe that a mature psychological and archetypal position can also be regarded as essentially secular. In this, science plays its part in revealing and de-mystifying the metaphors and intuitions we already know to be true, whilst unveiling yet new layers of mystery and inquiry.

These metaphors of narrative and myth, from the great poetic and spiritual traditions, are intuitions of truth. The people who told these stories did not have the means to test their ideas. Yet they provided us with ways of asking new questions and understanding our world – and of gathering the scattered notes into a harmony and refrain.

We are back to stories again – we always return to stories!

Symphonies as stories. Songs as stories. Poems as stories. Dreams as stories. Morality tales. Narratives of our lives. Cultural histories and identities, and the common ground that exists between us that far outweighs the superficial differences. Stories that remind us of the inevitability of the fall of civilisations. Tales that remind us of the frailty and nobility of human beings at their best.

Superficial myths are just fantasies of wishful thinking. In contrast, the deep mythologies that draw on the archetypal world that every human shares contain the stories that will ultimately redeem us.

Evolution of a psyche

Evolutionary psychology suggests that our patterns and behaviours are expressions of our latent heredity. Facial expressions and triggers for emotion, for example, are common across the human species, and we are programmed to learn our native language with inbuilt templates common to us all.[48] We may even have an inbuilt love for nature and our fellow living things (though we might easily miss it!) that Edward Wilson has termed 'Biophilia'.[49]

Carl Jung showed that our psychology also has a latency, manifesting as archetypal figures and stories. This does not contradict an evolutionary view. Taking an integral approach, the mind's unconscious, archetypal layer can be regarded as emerging from our biology. Jung's presentation of the great human symbols shows us how we make meaning from this deepest layer of mind. This is the shared patterning that underpins our personal and cultural experience.

Overlaid on this is a vast, unconscious storehouse of memorabilia and myth that Guy Claxton calls the 'habit map'.[50] This habitual structure allows us to navigate our daily lives without getting lost in our inner worlds. However, we all know it is possible to become so preoccupied with habit that our lives become joyless.

Psychotherapy clients may complain: *"I've fallen into a rut"*, or *"I know there's something more"* or *"I've got to where I wanted to get in my life but I'm just not happy"*. When living becomes habitual like this, we can lose sight of our place in the wider drama of existence. In doing so we risk losing the depth and richness that lies at the heart of a full and joyful life.

There is a shadow-side to developing archetypal intelligence. Exploring deep places and dangerous stories can be terrifying, yet is essential for a fulfilled and engaged life. Only by facing up to all that emerges from our mind, body and soul can we be truly free.

All psychology is essentially archetypal. We cannot understand human behaviour without understanding our shared archetypal inheritance. We cannot 'make souls' without understanding that everything we do happens in the swirl, tug and pull of the giant archetypal waves that circle our worlds.

Allowing ourselves to be carried by these waves, even learning to surf these powerful giants, goes right to the heart of a joyful, fulfilling and humble human life.

The dreaming

Since childhood, dreams have been as significant to me as any other life event. For years I kept a journal of every dream and dream-fragment I remembered, and still write down the big ones: dreams that catch the breath and those that are vivid, lucid, unusual, grand and significant. On looking back, one childhood dream of terrifying power seems as significant as any 'real' event in shaping me. Much later, a numinous dream of a golden tower led me from a path I had been following in my adult life, towards a place I needed to be.

I am an adult who developed from the child I once was – but 'I' also emerge each morning from my pool of dreams. My dream history makes me, as much as memories from my 'real' past.

The boundary between dreams and life can seem permeable at times. Dreams aren't just symbolic images, but part of the essential phenomenology of life. Dreams are roads to the unconscious and keys to our body's wisdom. They are gateways to shared understanding and palaces where genius resides. They are places where we sort each day's trash and treats.

Dreams are puzzles, providing clues to our life story, soul's path and cultural truth. Dreams are where different layers and states of consciousness can co-exist in one luminous, extended moment.

In dreams, we may share worlds with others in ways that are not possible in the material world. In 'social dreaming' workshops, for example, when dreams are recalled and told, the dreamer gives voice to the many, and collective meaning can be revealed.[51]

Dreams capture each generation, asking questions rarely asked in our daytime world. In dreams, history breaks down and magic and meaning cross over to us, as if through a veil. We travel where there are neither boundaries nor a reliance on science or civilising psychology. More than any religion, dreams offer the ultimate challenge to science's claim to speak the one truth about existence. As James Hillman puts it, dreams are about *"making soul in the very midst of nature."* [52]

In some cultures, there is no divide between dreams and waking. It is from these Dreamtime communities that wisdom has been captured and held, and from where the essence of our human creativity and joy is often revealed.

Sharing the lucidity of our deeper dreaming can help us touch a collective truth of a different kind: one that is not unconsciously and blindly acted out. It is drawn out from our imagination and spun into the sky with all the colours of the rainbow.

Yet it sometimes seems that our civilisation acts out as if in a dream. What is accepted as logical and rational, at a distance, seems like surreal madness. In the context of our current economic, social and ecological lives, we are sleep-walking towards a fall.

There are some dreams that we need to wake up from.

Science of the soul

In dreams, the boundaries between objectivity and experience, physiology and psychology, metaphor and reality break down. In dreams, logic and the rule of time and the physical world collapse. And the body dreams too: through our physical experiences; our physiological emotions, intuitions and anxieties; our aches, pains and illnesses. Arnold Mindell calls this the 'dreambody': *"an entity that is dream and body at once – the 'absolute real personality."* [53]

Then there are the truths of objective science; the material phenomenology of our dreaming lives. Here, the biochemistry of dreaming and the physiology of sleep is explained. However, whilst this reality can be mapped, the content of our dreams cannot.

Stuart Hameroff speculates that consciousness and dreams might operate at a quantum level. In this view, they are not contained within the boundaries of a personal psyche: *"In the quantum world there are deep interconnections and multitudes of possibilities. Time doesn't exist. In some sense our unconscious dream world is a lot like the quantum world. In fact, dreams may actually occur in the quantum world. It's not a different dimension, just the other side of our everyday reality."* [54]

So in this age of the quantum dream, can there be a science of the soul? We have evolved to be animals who experience both soul and spirit, yet rationalists claim there can be no ghost in the machine. Dispelling the spiritual, they argue, liberates humanity from the historical chains of religion and superstition.

Yet, out goes the baby with the bathwater. Dreams are ghosts. They don't come from 'God', but from the gods of our imagination.

There can be no real resolution to the debate about the ghost in the machine vs. the evolved machine. Phenomenologically – biologically – we evolved as existential animals that experience spirit and are conscious of soul. Our dreams, imagination and contemplation *always* carry meaning.

We have animal minds that construct elaborate metaphors to explain why we are here. One of these metaphors insists on rationalism. The idea of a spiritually empty machine, alone in the world, with only one life-span, is as rich with meaning as any ghost or god our dreams might conjure up.

Letters from home

"So may you have dreams that save you from yourself
And I wish you dreams that take you far into mysteries
And I wish you dreams that show you the things you need to see that will help you
And I wish you dreams that will please your ear and comfort you
And I wish you dreams, especially, that are direct, sweet, loving letters from home"
(Clarissa Pinchola Estes, 1993)[55]

For the religious, dreams are visions opening a relationship with God. A saviour is projected into the world, imagination is closed down and mythical experience channels down one 'true' path. The projection is freeze-framed. This one truth becomes the only truth. No-one else's imagination (or different God) can match the cultural potency of a revealed truth and a shared faith, blindly experienced.

Dreams, for me, are more potent and personal than any God. If we are prepared to live with uncertainty and ambiguity, dreams open up a deep relationship with self and world; for the dreamed-of saviours, gods and ghosts are poetic and creative images that constantly emerge and re-emerge in different ways.

These are whispered voices of a true self of many parts (and in the dream realm the self *does* equate with soul!). They are guides to the sometimes brutal, collective truth of humanity. The archetypal truth of dreams is that everything about being human can be encapsulated without boundaries, gravity, rationality or logic.

So, the poet regards dreams as magical receptacles of depth and mystery, and the poet would be right. The psychotherapist sees hints and metaphors of a soul being made – and she is also right. For the scientist, dreams are evolved functions of a complex brain, and this view also holds true.

The ways in which archetypes and metaphors manifest themselves in dreams provides us with the material by which we can begin to understand ourselves and the contexts of our ecology. Dreams have always carried clues to these understandings. They are often the first places we look when asking ourselves big questions.

Yet this loops us back to an old battle between the different gods of truth – between objectivity, subjectivity, spirit and science.

Perhaps we could think differently about dreams and the magic that emerges from them? Maybe the simple trick is not to explain their hows and whys, but just learn to experience them fully. Then we can observe them with wonder and live out this part of our lives with joy. And if we are joyous dreamers, it may help us live our waking lives with passion, love and understanding.

Perhaps this is what Clarissa Pinchola Estes meant by wishing us *"sweet, loving letters from home"*?

Interlude: Looking forward

First there is hope and clarity; at other times clouded vision and confusion. The paradox of the future is that it has not yet happened – but is, in some way, more real than the past. When we imagine a better world and a more authentic life for ourselves we often evoke this reality. We think of a future for our family, work and community; of pains and future glories.

Though the future can give hope, it can also be an escape route from the present – a way of always wanting more and never being satisfied – and therefore it carries fear.

The imagined future is one I may have constructed from my past and my psychology, but there is a touch of the wished-for, 'never-never' about it. Always striving, always seeking. What would the world be like without a future to hope for?

However, the future is also in the hearts and minds of those who wish to destroy. We do not share their hope. Vision is all very well, but if it carries destruction and evil, what then? Isn't this future a dangerous chimera, promising all, but blind to the fact that much we already have is precious? The future is too important to be left to grand visions of change, personal fulfilment or the glory of the gods.

So, the future makes me restless and holds the light of promise. Perhaps I need a more down-to-earth utopia – one which stands a little sifting and scratching? To envision my future more humbly, I might need a more grounded, archaeological imagination.

In her visionary book *'Always Coming Home'*, Ursula LeGuin reflects on how she can construct an *"archaeology of the future"*, imagining and reaching people who *"might be going to have lived a long, long time from now"*.

She writes: *"the only way I can think to find them, the only archaeology that might be practical, is as follows: You take your child or grandchild in your arms, or borrow a baby, not a year old yet, and go down to the wild oats in the field below the barn. Stand under the oak on the last slope of the hill, facing the creek. Stand quietly. Perhaps the baby will see something, or hear a voice, or speak to somebody there, somebody from home."* [56]

What is she saying? Perhaps this:

If we see the future as if through a baby's eyes, if we keep a humble ear to the earth, if we treat the future as we should our past (with the love and tenderness it deserves), if we envision the ways in which others might choose to live, rather than how we would like them to live – then the future can be our friend after all.

Part 4 notes and references

45. *The Beast in the Nursery* by Adam Phillips (Faber and Faber, 1998)

46. *A Way of Being Free* by Ben Okri (Phoenix, 1998)

47. Quote from *The Lost Coast* by Drew Kampion (Gibbs Smith, 2007)

48. Cross cultural research on emotions and facial expressions is summarised in *Emotions Revealed: Understanding Faces and Feelings* by Paul Ekman, (Phoenix, 2006). The inbuilt templates for language learning are described in *The Language Instinct: The New Science of Language and Mind* by Steven Pinker, (Penguin, 1995).

49. Biophilia is a concept defined in *The Future of Life* (Little, Brown, 2002) by Edward O. Wilson as: *"The innate tendency to be attracted by other life forms and to affiliate with natural living systems".*

50. Guy Claxton's books on the unconscious, its functions and cultural interpretations, and creativity-based education include: *The Wayward Mind: A History of the Unconscious* (Little, Brown, 2005) and *Be Creative: Essential Steps to Revitalise Your Work and Life,* with Bill Lucas (BBC Active, 2004), in which the concept of the 'habit map' is described.

51. Social dreaming is a field of action research and practice that connects people and social systems through their shared dreams: *"One can think of the world as composed of an infinite number of social systems, in each of which there is an unattended parallel social system, of free thoughts, musings in the mind, fantasies and dreaming, streams of consciousness, unencumbered by conscious logic. Every person who participates in these parallel systems has dreams. They may be forgotten or regarded as so much junk mail to be discarded. But we know that people dream. The dream is a particle version of the dreaming that goes on all the time, as a wave. Social Dreaming can be understood or seen as having, engaging in, the unattended part of the discourse of a social system, a bringing of it into conscious reflection".* Quote from: http://socialdreaming.com

52. Quote from *Re-Visioning Psychology* by James Hillman (HarperPerennial, 1992): *"To return dreams to nature by measuring their images against natural events misses the extraordinary intensification of fantasy. It misses the fact that dream and fantasy, and symptoms too, are making soul in the very midst of nature".*

53. *Dreambody: The Body's Role in Revealing Itself* by Arnold Mindell, (Penguin 1982). For practical ways of applying Mindells's ideas, see also *Working with the Dreaming Body* (Penguin, 1985).

54. Quote from Stuart Hameroff's website that also carries a range of papers, articles and references on his work on 'quantum consciousness', and in particular his theory developed with physicist Roger Penrose: *"The basic idea is that consciousness is, in itself, a transition between the quantum and everyday classical worlds. So it isn't so much that the conscious observer causes a 'collapse of the wave function', as it's called. Rather, consciousness IS a collapse – a particular type of self-collapse. Consciousness is a process on the edge between the quantum world and our everyday world. I get this funny image in my head of someone – me, I guess, but anyone – surfing on the edge, like a wave breaking between the two realms"* from www.quantumconsciousness.org

55. Quote from: *The Beginners's Guide to Dream Interpretation* by Clarissa Pinchola Estes (audio)(Sounds True, 1993).

Interlude: Looking forward

56. *Always Coming Home* by Ursula LeGuin (Grafton, 1988), has been a key book for my emerging integrative understanding of soul-making, creativity and culture. In it, she imagines how the lives of people living thousands of years in the future might be seen by history or anthropology. She shows, in this unique novel, how poetry, lifestyle, metaphors and myth emerge directly from the cultural connection with an ecological 'self' that, in twentieth century western culture, had been largely lost. There's more about the world of *Always Coming Home* at her website: http://www.ursulakleguin.com/

Part 5
Pieces of joy

Presence

Wrap yourself in this moment like an old grey blanket on a cold winter's day.
Look closely at this flower – its petals, stem and stamen –
Then see farther than you've ever seen.

Listen closely to the rustle and whisper of the world beneath the traffic's rumble.
Let the wind brush your cheek and reach out to touch the air with your fingertips.
Smell the silence, taste the sweet presence, go on living.

In praise of joy

The hoar frost settles on a grey, damp, winter townscape and it won't lift, I think, for some days. The day is bleak and chilled, with nothing much to recommend it. People shuffle about in coats and scarves never quite feeling warm enough.

This is how it is for us: we live in a frozen world; there are financial crises, ecological implosions, wars spluttering into life. People fear the future and concern themselves with the habitual surface of things.

I find myself on the hopeful side of the street. I am a little surprised by this, and thankful to the people who love and sustain me and make this possible. I am also grateful to be open to moments of joy and wholeness that give me a sense of perspective on my world. For the time being, it seems possible to hope; to see through to my creative self and live with a sense of space and silence.

One thing that characterises hopelessness is an inner clamour and conflict about how we 'should be' in the world. Another is a layer of watchful, anxious need that seems to settle on our lives (like the hoar frost). This freezes and muffles passion and calling and renders our deeper dreams and wishes opaque, obscure and unattainable.

Yearning and despair emerge from one-dimensional, cultural myths that tell us how we should live our lives. These injunctions give twisted meaning to what has the potential for wisdom and beauty.

Joy doesn't depend on what we tell ourselves we are supposed to be doing. Rather it is based on simple, wholesome practice: good work, meaning, love, a sense of presence – and woven through, an emerging sense of a soul being made. These, along with a trust in our own inner direction and growth, can make all the difference.

On some days, doubt, fear, anger, ambition, pride, blame, self-doubt and hopelessness will get in the way of such presence. The way to experience joy and appreciate beauty is to allow our attention to come through this difficult emotional terrain. Though this is a simple idea, it is a profoundly difficult piece of disciplined lifework.

Joy is not a permanent state – it is transient and changeable – and all the more splendid for this. We should recognise that bleakness and despair are also transient. Joy is possible if despair is faced and ultimately resisted through our activism, love and engagement.

One day soon, the hoar frost will give way to crisp, bright winter sunshine. Spring and all its promise will be in the air.

Belonging

Once I belonged in my hometown, where my clumsy, muddled adolescence took place. When I look back to those days, the memories of the misfit I felt I was can still tighten my soul. Further back, in childhood, I belonged in a village where my memory plays out in a golden age of nostalia. A place where I roamed lanes and fields, and embedded myself in a memoried landscape.

Neither place holds my belonging now. Many miles and decades from these places, I sense that belonging can lie in giving up old attachments and painful associations. Belonging must be where I am. Joy comes from being fully in a place and making it mine – if only in this moment.

Those of us lucky enough to live with the cultural luxury of a holiday, sometimes look around us at the beautiful place that has enticed us, and say, *"I could live here!"*. This is more than just a wish to escape from our frantic, speed-driven lives. There can sometimes be a hint of rightness carried in a place – a kind of fit. Fundamentally, the joy of belonging is the sense that we belong with ourselves. When we strip away the yearning, anxiety and speed, this can be anywhere.

Somewhere on the mid-point on my diagonal journey through life, I found myself in a new town: belonging, for a while, in a family and community of my own.

Then, years later, there was a holiday when we drove across a bridge that spanned a stream that ran through a small, breathtaking moorland. We turned and drove into a village, a few miles from the sea, into another belonging.

Finding and re-finding a sense of belonging over a lifetime can be like archaeology: carefully scraping away the layers to find a truer embedding. Though we may yearn for the past or wish for the future, true belonging emerges as much from imagination and sensed connection as in the actual place.

Belonging finds me here in a quiet room in the late afternoon. My children are grown, my granddaughter is born, my wife works quietly near to me in this old Granary we have rebuilt together.

Today I belong here. I have let go of yearning, nostalgia and obligations. This is a place of life, purpose, love and tenderness. A belonging with the sharp, familiar promise of the salted west-wind and winter beaches.

Dispossession

For descendents of Africans wrested from their homelands, belonging holds a different type of yearning. For them, salted winds were not gentle breezes playing on beaches and harbours, but roaring storms tossing ships on the high seas, with human cargos in their holds.

For those who live in new lands with legacies of racism and genocide, their distant belongings – even when separated by thousands of miles and generations of ancestors – can be the ones that feel real. The ghetto has a paradoxical romanticism. It holds belonging, longing and a collective memory for those who have been dispossessed.

The yearning of exile is born from greater suffering than I can imagine. People look to Africa, Israel, Palestine for their belonging and history – and to touch a fractured cultural soul. Belonging to somewhere or someone offers a hint of joy to those whose life and history has not been joyful. Yearning is poignant, but seldom holds joy. It is only when a dispossessed soul is able to feel free in a new place that true belonging can take root.

In past centuries, most people lived without any sense of the freedom that many of us now take for granted as a birthright. For them, belonging was assumed. It was embedded in the earth, in the village or tribe, and in a community of belief. Most of all, belonging was carried in stories. People belonged (as we all do deep down) in a 'Dreamtime'. Yet the irony is that even when we are 'free' and 'awakened', we still yearn for this deeper belonging.

If belonging lies in stories, we might say that all fiction is about this deep sense – much of poetry too. For some, the joy of belonging is in telling their stories from within a cultural community or in the presence of their God.

The rationalist response to this is to regard such faith as delusional and superstitious. Yet often these stories are psychological responses to un-belonging, broken families, dispossession and ruptured communities. Without necessarily taking on the religious or cultural assumptions of these dispossessed peoples, we can search this territory of yearning and un-dampened spirit for clues to how we might all feel at home.

Few psychological or political projects have ever been undertaken that carry the solidarity that this implies. All humans want to belong, and we all want to be free. We might argue that until everyone has the freedom to live in the place they call home, no-one can fully belong anywhere. Coexistence, equality, cultural acceptance and healing are all prerequisites to belonging.

Grief flares up

"I sit looking out of the window. Outside, beyond the garden, is a sunset almost too beautiful to describe in words. The colours in the sky change moment-by moment, clouds glowing orange as the sun passes behind them, igniting so they seem to flare, then die down and glow like embers. Above this fiery horizon the sky is soft silver-blue and against it, the trees stand utterly still – silhouetted green. I will sit here as dusk falls, and watch the blossom in the garden glow in that way flowers do on early summer evenings. Like little lamps sitting in the grass and hanging from the bushes. In this moment I realise what I am grateful for."

A few days before I wrote these words, a colleague and friend had died. She was one of those people who had a quality of engagement that meant everyone who knew her had a story to tell. Her funeral was a celebration yet, as always in these circumstances, she was lost to her people far too early.

Grief is such a pure, essential emotion. At its cleanest, it is pain distilled to an essence; a hurt so keen and poignant that disintigration seem inevitable. It is no wonder we fear it, whilst Pema Chödrön is still able to write: *"Things falling apart is a kind of testing and also a kind of healing."* [57]

It may be necessary for grief to be cleanly experienced so we can move on in our lives and with our loss. It may also be necessary so that we can do justice to our humanity in an unjust and difficult world.

This is a key issue for our age; the acknowledgment of grief is a symbol of our cultural dignity. How many of us own up to sorrow, even when we have something tangible to grieve for? Even those of us who lose someone seem have a cultural limit set on our grief. This loss is such an enormous thing, yet what we hear is: *"Move on, get over it, do not show, do not feel..."*.

The world can be a grim place and we all lose something or somone along the way. Yet we deny, hide or curtail our grief, so those who feel loss most keenly do not feel entitled to show it.

The cultural reality is that grief has its limits; yet how can we live life if we do not live grief? How can we live life if we do not hold what we have lost in our hearts? How can we live life if we do not face up to the reality of our own ending?

At the end of the day, I wrote: *"The sun has gone now and the light it left has brushed the horizon with a wash of fading pink. The blue in the sky is darkening and the trees are black against it, the flowers have faded and will hide their light now till morning. Will I feel grief for the loss of this day – so flawed, yet so perfect in its ending? If only we could all die like this!"*

On vulnerability

It came as bit of shock, although I know it shouldn't have done. Here I was, sitting alongside people, encouraging them that it was OK for them to be open to pain in order to experience joy. Then my vulnerability floored me.[58]

I'd done this stuff for a while; based it on a simple wisdom that in order to be fulfilled I should be open to vulnerability. I encourage my clients to widen their parameters, to put away certainty and deal with pain by facing it. Yet all the time there was a narcissistic piece of me thinking I had it sorted.

Surely I should have seen this coming? I've done my hours in therapy, training and groups. I'd got myself a little theory that seems to hang together. I have embarked on a big adventure with my wife of over thirty years, have great relationships with my grown-up children, and have seen my work and creativity bloom as never before.

Like all of us, I have some cultural myths to contend with. The clinical myth that we can all be fixed. The scientific myth that we can know the workings of the 'mind'. The spiritual myth that we are all 'one with the universe'. And, finally, the insidious, personal myth of the healer: that I can be both humble servant and guru.

So, on waking from the fantasies these myths had elicited, I realised I had been brought up short by my shadow, while my soul sniggered affectionately in the background!

The pressure had been building for a few weeks. New ideas, poems, projects and future schemes were bubbling up. There was the promise (and anxiety) of a new home, and the worry of finances coming together at the right time. Ventures, developments, collaborations – all flooding through my mind and threatening to overwhelm me.

And I felt a deep responsibility for those who depend on me: my clients, family, and the partners I work with on these creative projects.

Yet below it all, there was a still, small voice whispering insistently; waking me as if from a dream. It reminded me that all this activity, change and transition was supposed to have a gentle purpose: that I would turn to the sea and try to live a sparce, clean life. Here, amidst the soft breezes and beauty, is where my creativity and calling lies.

So, I re-committed to my soul-making with as much self-compassion as I could muster. Somehow I had forgotten that one purpose of vulnerability is to question the headlong rush towards new excitement!

And the joy of vulnerability is in its reminder to us that fulfilment is not about heading onwards and upwards. Vulnerability invites us to stay with the moment and go – if anywhere at all – inward and deep. It is the journey down that is the authentic route to freedom – or else, like Icarus, we will come to a fried and watery end!

If self is a location

"If self is a location, so is love."
(Seamus Heaney, 2006)[59]

I'm intrigued by the way the self is mediated by love. Not love by chance, but love believed in. This rests on a number of things: our history, beliefs and how open we are to the world. As Eric Fromm wrote fifty years ago: *"Is love an art? Then it requires knowledge and effort"*.[60]

My own work, and that of my clients to know themselves, has led me to this point. Knowledge of self is not an easy option; it takes time and can be painful. Yet opening ourselves to suffering is a sure-fire way to touch joy, and a key to this is in our willingness to let vulnerability into our relationships – for this is what love means.

If we love someone, then we think we should be able to trust them implicitly – yet in trusting we become vulnerable. This can help us know ourselves, but we also fear we will suffer when we are let down. This might be one reason why we sometimes fail to love openly and fully enough and, therefore, fail to feel sufficiently loved in return.

Though 'true love' might be the ideal, so often we struggle with what Seamus Heaney calls love's *"options, obstinacies, dug heels and distance"*.

Another dimension is found in the destiny we all carry within us, but can spend a lifetime struggling to follow. When we stray from this path of calling, we get stuck in places that others (including those we love) have constructed for us. We want to stay loyal to them, but feel the tug of calling pulling us in other directions.

This conflict makes it hard to love fully. It is a constant dance; a push and pull of different relationships with ourselves and others. David Whyte's idea of the 'three marriages' can help us with this awkward dance. We are married, he says, to 'Work', 'Self' and 'Other', and only when we recognise that each of these requires a commitment in itself, can we reconcile ourself to love.

The trick is in generosity and mutuality. *"To 'love' another,* he writes, *"...we must love the desires that the other person holds for the other two marriages. These desires are indicators of who our partner is at the moment and who the partner is becoming".*

Even though we may be confused and unsure about these two other marriages ourselves, it is the *"act of creating a conversation"* about them that is important. This *"helps us to understand the other's struggles and, importantly, to overhear ourselves say things we didn't realize we knew in our own lives."* [61]

All this requires love, commitment, a recognition of calling in ourselves and others and a good deal of practice over our lifetime. As Victor Frankl wrote, *"no one can become fully aware of the very essence of another human being unless he loves him";* [62] so it makes sense that we'll only feel love, when we learn the 'art of love' for ourselves.

On meeting

On meeting someone, I often fall in love. Don't misunderstand this. For a therapist (or any person truly meeting another) this is an necessary and essential part of knowing them as fully as possible.

There is little joy in applying logic and careful analysis to this first flirtation. Just find a piece of him or her that you can love and fall for it. Your heart – committed – will intuitively find the joyful places and paths to goodness, if they are there to be found.

Sometimes such a meeting, as we fall for one another, can bring surprises, smiles and connections. However it can also be perilous, so it might be wise not to commit ourselves too far, too soon!

We might know, for example, that we are susceptible to the subtle invitations of a charming, flattering man or woman. Knowing the boundaries of our self and our relational attachments can help us stay safe – but this should not stop us! We can still respond and, in doing so, bring out the best in them. As we go with their charm, we choose to move towards their better self; eventually to retreat with a rueful *"au revoir"*.

If this is done with love and humour, they will be left with a sense of the warmth we have brought to the encounter. Perhaps, they will even find a way of moving beyond the surface of their pleasing smiles to deeper, more fulfilling places?

When we are with someone for the first time, we can use the flow of our intuition to meet them. Otherwise we will miss the deep river in them, dismissing them as shallow or casting them as this type or that.

Their 'type' will emerge, but all we need to know about a person is already there in that first encounter.

Our intuition and our willingness to notice everything in this first meeting can tell us so much. Where their pain lies, what their avoidances look like, what touches their joy, what hold their passion – we listen for these. How they hold their body, breathe and walk into the room, how close they come. What their armour looks like when they protect themselves, how they fight – we watch for these. Above all we look for the ways they allow their vulnerability, and we allow our own without seeking advantage.

And my heart can sing and break, all at once, when I meet someone who, defying the temptation to close against pain or suffering, has opened their self to it.

Since I love you

In everyone's life there are people who are always connected to us; weaving through our time on earth, staying somehow constant, yet changing with us.

Sometimes the weave of this relationships is loose. A friend, once intimately met, may only enter our life from time to time, with a distance of months or years between. Yet it is as if these two souls know when is the right time to have their next conversation. The strands of their friendship go throughout their lives, often transcending other relationships – even marriages – and weathering many storms. Even when miles apart, these souls somehow find each other.

For others the fabric of the relationship is more closely knit. Two people spend their days together; find it natural to be together, hard to be apart. They may be partners, spouses, sisters, brothers, children, grandchildren, friends. There is a proper rhythm for our relationship with this person – one that is just right and there for the right time.

There can be a number of such people in our life – or just one. They can come early and stay with us for a long time, or they can meet us at any time during our life. The soul's task for us is always just to notice them and not turn them away.

Meeting and sustaining soul friendship is the highest ideal of the social, relational self. It involves us in meeting another in dimensions that go beyond the everyday. The mundanities of ordinary life have their relational equivalents in the kinds of surface friendships that go nowhere, or that operate within boundaries of narrow assumption and expectation.

We all may have lost soul friends through our inability (or unwillingness) to love them as they were like nobody else. The important thing is not to turn this into a habit. To recognise where the patterns of moving towards and moving apart have become too established, and to allow these two souls to weave through and around one another.

John O'Donohue told us a beautiful name for this friendship from the Celtic tradition – the '*anam cara*'[63] – and he quoted a line from Pablo Neruda that says it all: *"You are like nobody since I love you."*[64]

On touching

In her dream, I reached out and touched her hand. She wishes deeply for this, yet is angry with me for not just listening to her repeated stories and deconstructions of the events of her life.

In the session that follows, this act of touching is offered for the first time and makes a promise to the quiet whispering of her soul. It kindles a flicker of joy in the child inside her. But she freezes. Her mind does not lack courage but her body does, and she is unable to respond to the offered hand.

Sometimes the remembered touch is not gentle. Remember, the child says, the rough and tumble of sibling wrestling. Remember the touch that was hurtful and cruel – or the one that was never there at all. Remember the ways that touch can punish and remind us of our allotted place in the world. The body remembers.

Children love a loving touch, yet as they grow can learn to avoid it as a defence against hurt. Loving or not, to be touched is to be vulnerable. It is as if the space around our skin is a invisible barrier between fear and safety. Choose safety, and our bodies yearn for love. Allow fear, and our body remembers life and its embodied traumas and refusals.

One day we yearn for the touch that unfreezes; opening us to our relational human-ness. Closeness. Contact. A hug. A supporting pat on the shoulder, a loving stroke on the bare skin. We find that sometimes the surrender to another's simple offering of touch is necessary.

Perhaps it can be done this way:

First learn to touch the world – its breezes, lifeforms, sun and spiking rain – and let it touch you.
Do this every day. Begin to breath deeply.
Start to clear your mind and body of your lifelong habits of refusal.
Do this every day. Be gentle with yourself.

After practicing this simple meditation (perhaps for several years!) you will be ready to be opened. Then you can meet the eyes of the person who offers you love.

Tentatively reach out your hand to meet their proffered touch. Magically, simply, soulfully, you feel their fear and freedom. Longing and dreams burst into waking life and lightning strikes you blind.

Life presents a new possibility: that trust in another's physical presence can bring you joy.

The gateway

"For sexual love to be an experience of true erotic pleasure, it must be imbued with beauty...and express the longings of the soul."
(Bruno Bettelheim, 1985)[65]

Ken Wilber once told an audience that, in the Tibetan Buddhist tradition, 'nirvana' can be achieved in two ways. First, through the sexual congress of two lovers, and second through the gateway of 'bardo', the transitional state between one life and the next. He tells a great teacher who chose the second way, eschewing the temptations of the conjugal gate. Wilber laughingly doubts this wisdom, commenting that this seems an overly earnest and joyless route! [66]

Perhaps the old scholar had a point? Sex is a temptation. A literal, not simply a moral route down. And in our culture, sex can often be so joyless and shallow. The industries that promote it – prostitution, pornography, advertising, fashion – are riven through with exploitation, abuse and cynicism. Meanwhile, sex is almost the only rite of passage remaining to adolescents. It is not celebrated and ritualised, however, but takes place frantically and sometimes violently in dark corners.

Sex cannot be ignored if we are to write of human fulfillment. Those who live with both Eros and Psyche, share passion, love and mutual respect. Sex sits alongside, perhaps surpasses, other peak experiences. We don't have to be a tantric adept or self-absorbed aficionado of sexual technique to know this. It's a fine line: writing about sex is expressing an opinion about it – taking a position, so to speak!

The erotic – Eros – is the loving touch, the captured glance, the glimpse of the partially revealed. Eros is about beauty and feeling beautiful, fingertips caressing skin to leave burning traces. The poetry of love and sex is a literature of joy. Nowhere else do we find words so close to worship as we do in secular verses dedicated to the lover.

However we also we know that the shadow is embedded deep into our sexual lives. The impulses that drive us towards sex are paths to beauty – but also to pain, disappointment and betrayal.

We seem drawn by sex to the dark places. These are the promises of strange, fumbled excitements and ritualised eroticism. There are the dreams of silk-lined tents in the desert night and bath-houses deep beneath our cities. A long shadow is cast by our culture's obsession with body and coupling, with finding a lover, falling out and betrayal. We are fascinated by the cycles of celebrity sex lives that revolve around their narcissistic, public obsessions and – as captured hordes – we gape or follow.

The assignation

Undress me, lover! Undress me!
Under your glance I will rise like a
Vibrant statue on a black plinth
Towards which the moon drags itself like a dog.
(Juana de Ibarbourou, translated by Brian Swann, 1983)[67]

It is time to reclaim sex for joy; to remind ourselves of this deep marriage. To name love as a gateway to heaven. To re-make our love-making as passionate, mutual, mysterious, and intriguing. To see it as the way our bodies, minds and souls can flow into one another.

The joy in love? The lover writing poetry. The couple losing themselves in each other, falling madly in love – being mad. The chance encounter. Feeling the ecstatic extremes of pain and joy.

The joy of sex (there I have used the phrase!) is always at the edge – always a balancing act. The most dangerous – and joyful – part of sex is that it is about desire. We see it in the eyes of the other, and at that moment nothing else matters except your eyes meeting mine.

Seen from the outside (despite the labours of eroticists and pornographers) sex is mundane, clumsy and comical. We laugh at sex precisely because we know both how ridiculous and joyful it can be.

Our positions around sex are fraught with danger, doubt and desire; scored through with possibilities, jealousies and renewals. Marriages remain unconsummated, long partnerships see passion fade. Sex can be a lode-stone for how we meet one another's need – or else disappoint. It is, in short, a barometer of the climate of our relating.

As soon as sex is pinned down we realise the truth that, in the wider scheme of things, it matters not a jot.

As Adam Phillips puts it: "*All prophets of the erotic are false prophets because every couple has to invent sex for itself. They are not so much making love as making it up. In our erotic lives uncertainty is delight, our awkwardness is passion.*"[68]

The myth of the 'practiced lover' is simply that – a myth. When an insecure man asks his lover "*was that good?*", the question is irrelevant. In that moment, any question is irrelevant. Yet we ask, because we have in our mind the kind of god or goddess we think we should be – or be with.

With sex, our imaginations truly run away with us!

Part 5 notes and references

57. Quote from, *When Things Fall Apart: Heart Advice for Difficult Times* by Pema Chödrön (Shambhala, 1997).

58. One of the contemporary champions of vulnerability is Brene Brown. She became known for her a TED talk given in 2010 called the *Power of Vulnerability* (http://www.ted.com/talks/brene_brown_on_vulnerability), and is the author of *Daring Greatly: How the Courage to Be Vulnerable Transforms the Way We Live, Love, Parent, and Lead* (Porfolio Penguin, 2013).

59. Quotes from poem: *The Aerodrome* by Seamus Heaney in *District and Circle* (Faber and Faber, 2006).

60. *The Art of Loving* by Eric Fromm (Thorsons, 2010 – reissue).

61 *Three Marriages: Reimagining Work, Self and Relationship* by David Whyte (Riverhead Books, 2009).

62. *Man's Search for Meaning* by Viktor E Frankl (Rider, 2004, new edition).

63. *Anam Cara: Spiritual Wisdom from the Celtic World* by John O'Donohue (Bantam Press, 1997).

64. Quote from poem: *Every day you play...* by Pablo Neruda, quoted in *Anam Cara* (see above), online at: http://hellopoetry.com/poem/every-day-you-play/

65. Quote from: *Freud and Man's Soul* by Bruno Bettelheim (Fontana, 1985)

66. You'll have to trust me on the Ken Wilber story, as the video concerned is not available online at the time of publication!

67. Quote from the poem *The Assignation* by Juana de Ibarbourou (translated by Brian Swann) in *In the Pink: Poems Chosen by the Raving Beauties from the Show* (The Womens Press, 1983). The show in question was a cabaret of women's poetry and song shown on the first evening of Channel 4 on November 2 1982. On their website, http://www.ravingbeauties.co.uk, they write: *"Raving Beauties was born out of a deep sense of frustration with domesticity, naivete and a burning need for a creative outlet. It led to an enormous personal, political and professional learning curve. We're still on it."*

68. *Monogamy* by Adam Phillips (Faber and Faber, 1996).

Part 6
On being free and crumbling

The fixing of things

I write and here it stays, on the page where it belongs.
I spit out words of every tongue, one by one.
I take exception, seethe, explode – to no avail;
it changes nothing, so long as minds stay fixed.

Chair, book, planet – these are solid words,
unlike love, quantum, faery, dream, singularity.
On this page I will oppose the fixing of things,
the clunking, bolting down of the world.

In this sense, mathematics and poetry are bedfellows:
enemies of the solid state, of literal, blind belief – and of sanity.

In the present tense

Dennis Potter was interviewed by Melvyn Bragg on Channel 4 in April 1994. He said: *"The only thing you know for sure is the present tense, and that nowness becomes so vivid that, almost in a perverse sort of way, I'm almost serene."* [69]

At the time, he was desperately ill with cancer and in the interview he has an ecstatic clumsy grace. On the one hand, dying, he says what he pleases; eloquent and rapier-like, he targets the political and intellectual culture of that time. On the other, with no constraints remaining within himself (with no sense of a future self), he is utterly free in the present.

The ultimate freedom for any individual is to be so much in the present that we notice precisely what is around us, free of any fears about the projected consequences of this 'moment'. Incidentally, this may be the only way to be happy and to make a difference in the world! The great writers, thinkers and activists were, in the main, unafraid for their personal futures. They were able to live in their own present and deep in the imagination of the people they inspired.

Presence comes together when the world and the multiple aspects of our 'self' come together. It is there when our three circles of energy (as Patsy Rodenburg calls them) flow through us. These circles define our energetic relationship to the world. The first is *"introspective and reflective"*; the third is *"outward-moving and non-specific"* and the second circle – holding it all together – is the *"energy of connecting."* [70]

There is a meditative quality to this, and meditation and presence are spiritual practices of deep wellbeing and connection. Such compassionate discipline allows our mind to connect all the levels of experience and self: past, future, internal, external, material and imaginary – all encapsulated in a moment of presence.

The ultimate joy of presence is in its simplicity. With practice, meditation can become deeper and more sustained, but *anyone* can have access to a sense of present wholeness if they are open to it! The starting point is simply to notice what is, and choose a context in which your presence is most available and emerges most spontaneously.

For me, one such place is a walk or run along the two miles of Newgale beach at low tide. Here, I always notice. Here, the wind always seems to blow away any troubled thoughts. Here, I feel that I, and the world, can be healed.

These moments may not be sufficient for a lifetime of deeper meditative presence to emerge. But this intuition also tells us that, whatever our life history and context, presence is always available to some extent. And there are times when life just seems more real.

This, as Dennis Potter recognised, is presence too: *"the nowness of everything is absolutely wondrous"*, he said, *"The fact is that if you see the present tense, boy do you see it; and boy can you celebrate it, you know?"*

A way of being free

Is it possible to hold a hope for a future in which we've made a difference? Perhaps this is where the political and psychological come together. Perhaps it is in the healing of the fracture between these two realms that freedom will come?

I don't get a sense, when I look at politicians, that many of them are really capable of being free. They are so bound up with fears for their short-term future and for the peculiar status that is so central to them being successful and influential. They are not unique in this, nor is it entirely their own fault. The rules of the game don't allow them any other way of being (except, I guess, to choose not to be a politician!).

To be truly free, we'd look back at our young selves with self-compassionate disdain; seeing our past self for who he or she was, without any need to defend or justify. That's not to say we won't have more mistakes to make. However, we can make a choice to face and live with our demons.

We can acknowledge that poetry, psychology and politics (by which I mean the ways we make each other free, rather than suited and booted game-play), are played out in the same deep, archetypal space. This is a world, writes Ben Okri, that *"does not necessarily yield up to the poetic"*; in which *"the poet needs to dwell in odd corners, where Tao is said to reside."*

It is not just poets who need to sit for a while in these dark places. All of us fear shadows and turn aside from freedom; in the process becoming *"separated from our true selves."* [71]

Stories of freedom hold our culture's imagination less than they once did and seem like historical whimsy to some. We also seem to have less of a sense of our psychological and cultural archaeologies (the ways our personal and social pasts collide in the present with the collective and political).

These intuitive understandings are essential to our individual and collective freedom and humanity. They carry justice and deep sanity forward in ways that are transformed into wisdom.

So I hope we are not too late and have not lost the chance that once we had: to search inside ourselves, touch the world with magic and – as Okri tells us we must – find our own ways of being free.

Everything crumbles

In a magazine article, the band Radiohead were interviewed about making their 2007 album, '*In Rainbows*'. It is clear that this challenged more than just their creative talents. *"You're always trying to deal with the fact that you're a small crumbly piece of stuff when you write these songs, and maybe thats why the songs are good"*, reflected Thom Yorke, *"So you're always taking some poison or another. Perhaps that's what makes carrying on so hard. You make a record, you wake up – and start writing something new, and everything crumbles again."* [72]

On the same day I read this article, I discovered a film about American artist, Jerry Wennstrom. A prolific young painter, he destroyed all his work and gave away his possessions at twenty-nine years-old, beginning *"a life of unconditional trust, allowing life to provide all that was needed."* [73]

Only after living like this for fifteen years did he start to create art again, and to have a profound influence on others. In the film, he describes the act of destruction and surrender, and how this led to the art he now produces in this second phase of his working life; work that is deep, disturbing, highly personal and totally honest.

Wennstrom has gone beyond 'self'; his creativity is an act of surrender and, as he says in the film, *"you can't get there by way of will, intelligence and good intentions"*.

The creative act is a challenge to the self we send out into the world. This might seem to offer us happiness, but there is also a shadow side: the potential for us crumble! And it opens us up to important questions – and a further challenge.

Are people like Wennstrom and Yorke simply different from us? Are they separated out by their talent and their luck at being able to do what they love to make a living?

Wennstrom's story might tell us otherwise. He gave up everything completely before coming back completely. How many of us could ever imagine ourselves being that courageous? The darker truth is that there may be no other choice than to crumble.

What we might learn from this is that for human beings to be happy and fulfilled, creativity is always part of the picture. However, opening up to the joy of creating also reveals the dark places in our soul. After all, isn't this from where the best art and insights often emerge?

If we are lucky, our own surrender may not mean giving everything up like Wennstrom, but it will involve listening carefully to our calling. It will also mean being able to stay with ourselves and the task in hand when everything starts to crumble.

The creative self

A key facet of creativity is self-awareness – knowing where you stand. Others are having the courage to make room in life for the creative self, and allowing the flow that comes to us when we are truly in balance. When this happens we enter a focussed, timeless experience and become immersed in whatever task we are in. It feels harmonious, even transcendent – a kind of letting go.

The poet Christine Evans writes of this: *"I, too, am addicted to that concentration that destroys time, in which all thoughts stream to an inevitable point and it seems that all you need to do is go with it and the words will write themselves. Does it qualify as 'trance'? Awareness alters, certainly; the 'me' is less narrowly individual, but in a strange way more what I could be – richer."*[74]

Creativity needs to be played with, messed around with – but it's not just child's play. Maybe we need a balance between the free child we were, and the adult we now are? As grown-ups, we can call upon greater cognitive abilities, experience and vocabulary in the creative act – but being a 'clever' adult can get in the way of being a creative child! In growing, we learn what is acceptable and what is not, and sometimes we just to let go of this too.

David Whyte writes of another dimension of the creative self: *"Somehow, whatever creative powers we have in our work are intimately connected with our ability to remember who we were amidst the traumas and losses of existence."*[75]

Sometimes our most creative ideas and creations emerge from difficulties and crises. People can find deep creativity at times of loss, transition or challenge, and faced with insurmountable problems, we often find we fall upon a solution!

In our personal lives, when we lose someone, we find solace in creativity. Writing or reading a poem or drawing or viewing a picture can touch us and help us heal, and as we grow older, our creativity is always waiting. How creative we can be when we reach the crisis of mid-life!

We should also consider where creativity springs from. The source of our creativity is our unconscious mind. The flash of a good idea that comes out of nowhere; the unfolding of an idea, poem, picture or strategy. To tap our creativity to the utmost we need to get down to the deeper layers of our memory and mind.

We should also reflect on how our culture affects this dimension of our self. Our world is so complex and ever-changing, that we need a particular kind of creativity to respond to it. Sometimes our busy-ness can seem so out of touch with the world's basic rhythms and patterns.

To be creative, therefore, we need sometimes just to

STOP

Good work

Good work is work that meets the soul and, at the same time, meets the world. When we see a builder bounding up ladders lying precariously on roof panels, or an engineer tuning up a car engine, we may see a person in touch with a moment of calling.

No doubt, at other times, these people will suffer from the familiar doubt, boredom and temptations of modern life. In that moment, however, I watch them with an empathetic joy, and perhaps a little envy. For me, roof ladders – like nagging car-engines, throbbing turbines and balance sheets – are from parallel, alien worlds. They are familiar and recognisable as places other people inhabit, but nowhere I have ever belonged!

There is a simple formula that tells us that when our work is out of touch with our vocation, life becomes joyless and stressful. Doubt, anxiety and boredom are embedded in body and mind until, bent and cynical, we hit a crisis and break down. Or worse, we end our short lives knowing we never quite lived up to our potential.

This existential crisis of work is a modern luxury. Before this century – and still in many parts of the world – people had little or no choice in the matter. Yet, perhaps because they had not yet lost connection with the rhythms of earth and community, they sometimes intuitively found their way into their work or, if very fortunate, were born to it.

Good work is not just about vocation and calling. Physical labour, at its best, has dignity and strength in it – even a meditative quality. At worst, of course, work is exploitative and degrading. The extremes of slavery and wage exploitation have no vocation or meditation in them. In these situations, people have had to find other ways to find joy from a restricted repertoire, but often have no choice but to live short and brutal lives.

Despite this, honest labour can still be a joyful thing. When my mind is right and I am not fretting over things not yet done, or am free from the other anxieties of modern life, I can spend time cutting the hedge or chopping wood and feel I have done something small and decisive.

The irony is that many of us who work for years in non-manual jobs often yearn for a more physical life. In the absence of work on the land, we find it at a gym or on a surfboard, mountain-side, football pitch or aerobics class. Either way, after a hard day's work or evening's exercise, we finish with limbs aching and tiredness washing through our bodies. We may relax, share conversation and sit with some wholesome food and a glass of wine.

And then, as if after a long day's work in the fields, we might drift into sleep and feel a small piece of satisfaction at this completion.

Working into flow

Flow is not easy. It has to be worked on, worked into, sometimes forced. When present, the joy it brings is often more quiet and absorbing than celebratory. Flow is what we feel when we are deep in a task that holds the potential to touch on our calling and talents. Flow is there when we are aligned with our strengths, skills and soul. It has a rhythm, a sureness – sometimes a sweet exhilaration – though this is not essential for flow to be useful to us.[76]

One cold Tuesday morning I was resisting and doubting. I doubted whether the workshop I had been asked to deliver was a) what I really wanted to do and b) really much good anyway! Even though I had agreed to this contract, it felt, at six forty-five that morning, merely a kind of trial. I wanted to be free of it, to shake it off and refuse its entry into my day. Yet, as people do at times like these, I got into my cold car, and drove across country to be on time for an appointment with my doom!

A couple of hours later, the people in front of me had warmed to the theme, and were engaging with each other and with me. As people invariably do, when in flow, they started to produce nuggets of insight and wisdom about themselves and their teams. Moments of deep presence began to emerge – the characteristic of a community that has permitted love and connectedness. My flow was about being in the midst of this – conjuring it. As I opened myself wholeheartedly to this group, I felt my instinctive skill and knowledge emerge.

In *'Outliers'*, Malcolm Gladwell writes of the making of talent. He charts the contexts and accidents that lead to people being successful. It takes years of practice, he writes, to be good at something to the extent that success emerges. Whilst sticking at it is one key factor, however, being in the right place at the right time is another.

We are told a myth of genius: that only a few people have it as their birthright. Yet the word itself refers to an individual's spirit! All of us have genius waiting to emerge, but sometimes the conditions have to be right. *"Sometimes"*, Gladwell writes, *"genius is anything but rarefied; sometimes it's just the thing that emerges after twenty years of working at your kitchen table."* [77]

Flow is joyful because, when we are in its midst, we are doing what we are practiced at and what is in our fate to do. This doing is in line with our personality and strengths. In other words, it occurs when we work with our talents, follow our star, and work hard to develop our craft.

The flow of play

For the positive psychologist, flow is at the heart of wellbeing. Someone who is in flow – at least some of the time – is likely to experience what psychologists call 'optimal functioning' – even joy! For the poet there is deeper, underlying truth: that in functioning 'optimally', at the edge of what the world demands from us, we experience a deep sense of rightness in our *doing*, as much as in our *being* in the world.

Flow isn't just about work, it is playful too. Energetically, it has much in common with the absorbed child lost in imagination. Children spend more time in flow (perhaps functioning more 'optimally') than adults. Children naturally stretch themselves; yet can often be discouraged by peer group or family, and therefore get out of the habit.

Yet a child whose life is characterised by neglect or cruelty can nevertheless lose themselves in flow. Such activities can become part of a rescue package for the growing child or adolescent that helps them transcend the damaged self; helping them to move beyond suffering, and cultural and social constrictions. When a young black man responds to racism by rapping about it, he is – in a very literal sense – in flow. His words are intrinsically joyful, however militant or angry they might seem to others.

The boundaries between play and work are blurred by flow. Passions and hobbies become vocations at any stage of life. The flow of play gives meaning to an otherwise mundane work-life: the surfer from the land-locked city lives for the weekend when she drives to find her wave!

Flow is ultimately a creative process, taking us well beyond the boundaries of our socialised existence. It makes an irrelevance of the idea of work-life balance. Why would we wish to balance work and life, when this kind of work holds, in potential, our identity and vocation?

Flow carries our calling and our commitment, over the long term, to the joyful project of soul-making. It opens us to the world and to other people whose presence is touched by us. This is a social dimension of the authentic self that asserts that flow is more than just psychological balancing. It is a channel through which joy passes on its way through our life, with all its transitions and challenges.

A piece of ordinary magic

The more experience we have of life, and can see the limitations of emotion, the more we recognise that empathy is nevertheless a genuine piece of ordinary magic. It is a phenomenon that gives us access – however fleetingly – to the inner lives of others and makes the connection between human beings.

The potential for empathy is built into human beings (a bit like our capacity for language) and develops in our interactions with parents, carers, teachers and mentors throughout our lives. Recently, neuroscience has begun to explore the theory that 'mirror neurons' in the brain might carry our capacity for empathy.[78]

A human being without empathy is a dangerous thing. Thankfully, this is rare, but we all know people whose lack of connection with others becomes harmful through the consequences of their actions. It doesn't take a psychopath to destroy – just a personality with a reduced capacity for emotional connection. Unfortunately, we live in a civilisation in which such people have accumulated much of the moral, financial and political power.

On the other hand, a human being with a high degree of empathy, can be a helper of great skill and effectiveness – even a visionary – for empathy goes beyond helping. It forms the basis for an ethical framework by which we can learn to live good lives.

Empathy also protects us. If we are able to step into the psychological world of another, it can help us understand how their selfish actions make some sense in the light of their own inner life, character and experience. This does not mean we condone their behaviour; rather it helps us to set our own boundaries and avoid being drawn into their world. It invites us to assert our own wishes more clearly. Such 'boundaried empathy' is useful for dealing with difficult people who are manipulative towards us.

Living with a high degree of empathy, we can maintain more fulfilling relationships and are less likely to harm others or feel out of control. At a basic level, empathy is the ability to step into the emotional world of another human being (or animal!); and with empathy there is no need to find blame or fear vulnerability.

Yet it is a combination of elements that makes empathy so magical. It makes connections; not just in the way we understand another person's feelings, but in a more dynamic way. When it is present, something deeply moving – even spiritual – can pass between us. It is a kind of magic; an invisible, powerful sense of 'us' that is felt and communicated – a dialogue of souls, so to speak.

At its most profound, empathy extends way beyond two people. It moves into the world as a conversation without words with everyone and everything.

Living with a practice

"This is not a time to live without a practice. It is a time when all of us will need the most faithful self-generated enthusiasm."
(Alice Walker, 2006)[79]

My own practices are poetry, curiosity, conversation and a sense of meditative presence. These 'enthusiasms' I am filled with flow into the words I write and from the people I speak with. These energies, and the directions they take me, nourish my practice.

In the future, more will be known (as ways of knowing evolve), yet the poetic voice that emerges from the human soul will always seek ways to practice. I have sometimes thought of myself as a poetic materialist, and so have directed my practice to inherently deep and secular ways of being. For any person's good life, practice is crucial, and it sometimes seems that belief can get in the way of fulfilment.

Knowledge is good – albeit an incomplete portion of human experience – and comes from accumulated, tested evidence. Joy and spirit (also good) come from subjective experience and from disciplined, connecting practice. One can have all these things, and feel connected, loved and have morality, with no religious belief. If someone else takes some comfort from God or faith in a supernatural 'soul' then so be it; but it sometimes needs stating that belief is not a prerequisite to goodness, joy or practice.

Human wholeness comes from recognising the boundaries between inner and outer worlds; between virtue and shadow. It also emerges from an understanding of the difference between the 'enlightenment' of knowledge, and that which comes from pinning our hope on faith.

So, this is a manifesto for science *and* soul. Science asks us to trade in "*a supernatural soul for a natural soul*", as Daniel Dennet puts it.[80] Although I love mystery, I think I can work with this, for it makes life no less wonderful and joyful – and certainly no less moral.

Yet practice is what we do – large and small things that make our life more connected and real – and this is about spirit. Building and sustaining practice is doing something we feel calls us, mindfully and with purpose, time and time again.

These are things that feel right and real but also – crucially – connect us with the world we live in. Practice is necessary to ensure engagement and to meet the challenges of life. Rob McNamara writes: "*Ultimately, practice is part necessity and part inspiration. To understand and embody practice requires both.*" [81]

Most importantly, our practices must align with the world and the others that inhabit it. Whatever we do should be for the benefit of this wider community: practice as a deeply political and ecological act – a conscious piece of activism. This is self-help that takes a lifetime and joins up person, people and planet in a coherent, connected whole.

Choosing this could be a positive 'win-win'; equally the consequences of not doing could be disastrous. Alice Walker warns us of this when she writes: "*We will be doubly bereft without some sort of practice that connects us, in a caring way, to what begins to feel like a dissolving world*".

The spirit of soulmaking

Recently, I watched a new film about Alice Walker, the poet, novelist and activist. She is someone who embodies the twenty-first century soul. She has lived her life with depth and has seldom shied from the world's pain.[82]

Revisiting Alice Walker's books now, almost thirty years since first reading them, I find new layers that remind me that joy and anger must be held in any authentic life. Re-reading her tales of freedom, shot through with rage at what white 'civilisation' has done to the world, I have discovered a new question.

I ask myself: what kinds of souls do we need to build for our new century? Not tribal souls, for despite the ecological wisdom we may find in these cultures, the world must move on from their wars and factions. Not immortal souls either, for the religious, narrowing down of Nature to 'God' was always just a rationale for the colonisation projects of powerful men. And the rational 'enlightened' soul of reason is not sufficient either – for once science carefully reveals one layer of explanation for how the world is, another mystery is revealed!

So Fanny Nzhinga's question to her husband, Suwelo in Walker's book, '*The Temple of My Familiar*', cuts to the core of any therapist worth his salt: *"What good is a shrink who doesn't understand about spirits?"*. 'Spirits' are right in the deep heart of Fanny's world. They are there in her identity and the ageless, timeless dreaming that holds her human soul.[83]

Over recent years I have realised that my psychotherapy practice has become, fundamentally, one of soul-making. This work is about deep experience, stark existence, the peculiar vagaries of character, human and non-human connections, imagination, creativity and metaphor. There is almost nothing of diagnosis in this – I am not a clinician. People do not come to me for a cure but, hopefully, for the understanding I can have the courage to give them.

Alice Walker has always told us that there are barriers to soul-making and freedom; barriers that benefit the powerful. The rest of us, if we can't hack it, suffer from 'mental illness': problems created and perpetuated by centuries of having our souls narrowed to something that can be explained – by gods, by God, by Science – by the men who mediate these cultural mythologies.

There are barriers in our minds too – often layers of them – that prevent us from seeing that the things that make us unhappy are the same forces of influence that exploit humans, our fellow lifeforms and this beautiful world. This is what psychology has come to: mopping up a cultural mess with drugs, positive thinking and the questionable idea of happiness as a self-help project – rather than something that emerges from a life lived well and deeply.

Yet Alice Walker's life and words teach us that it is up to the soul-makers and shrinks amongst us to champion the spirits – even if we don't experience these in the same way as those who speak with them more directly. Our task is to sit with our vulnerability visible, nurture our humility and embrace our responsibility as soul activists for a new world.

The soul activist

Activism is often regarded as the special way a cultural or political identity is acted out. In this way of seeing, ordinary people are not activists; we just wait around until the battles have been fought by others, and get on with our lives again.

Yet, an activist is *anyone* who is actively engaged with their life, community and world. It may be as simple as that. True, *soulful* activism is the very opposite of partisan, flag-waving tribalism that promises to change the world, but often does so very little.

A soul activist might be any of us. Soul activists prepare for new realities, tell new stories and 're-mind' our culture. They help craft responses to social, cultural and ecological crisis that are up to the job. They re-connect what has been scattered through their art, work and inquiry. They help others by offering healing, clarity, courage, leadership, inspiration and counsel.

Perhaps the mark of a true soul activist is someone who will more often choose to cherish rather than change the world. They will not shy away from change when this is necessary and possible, but they are as likely to be involved in telling new stories as setting up a campaign office.

Philosopher Andrew Taggart has something important to say of this. when he writes: *"The world is not to be saved, for such is a category mistake. It is instead to be savored, its way manifested through our perceiving rightly, acting well, and expressing something properly."* [84]

So how do we know what to do? How can we avoid the pitfalls of avoidance, burn-out or choosing the dead-end option? How can we use our basic moral intuition to make the right choices: when to paint and when to protest?

For the soul activist, making these choices will be about timing: joining, so to speak, the dance of a movement just at the right time. This being so, we can only do this with a level of awareness of the possibilities flowing into and out of each step and action we take.

We should be clear that we cannot take action on the expectation that we will make change. We can only be authentic to our broad selves and deep connections, and have trust in what flows from these.

Sometimes this will be a seed falling on stony ground. Sometimes the season and soil will be more fertile. It will help us to have an intuition of this, so we don't end up railing against an unfair universe that doesn't receive our actions with gratitude. Soul activists, therefore, must maintain a sensitive awareness in order to to sustain our creativity and influence in whatever sphere we choose to apply it.

Much of this awareness and calling lies at an intuitive level, outside of our direct cognitive experience. A small poem might have more influence, in the long run, than banner waving demonstrations; and a piece of art, conjured from deep by a tentative, beautiful soul, do more to change perceptions than eloquent and partisan words spoken in a parliament, council chamber or campaign rally.

The soulmaking child

Imagine a single child who may grow to have a profound influence on the culture or politics of her nation or world. When she is small, she is still only a small child! In turn, the parents whose intuition whispers to them that this girl is special (and not JUST because she is their daughter), who start to nurture her calling and open her to her possibilities, are doing something special in their own right.

These parents are also soul activists. Their actions emerge from love close in, tempered with an intuition of something much bigger and grander beneath. Their little girl's future walk to freedom is carried in her growing acorn; and they hold the responsibility of her emergence in theirs.

They cannot know this, and she cannot know this – other than at the soulful, intuitive level that tells them all that this something is right and important to do. And the more her parents' own souls have been made, the more their intuition can be trusted and the more able they will be to help their son or daughter fly. This is difficult for them, as their protective instinct kicks in. Love often tells us to keep our children safe, rather than setting them free into the fateful hands of their calling!

Adults who champion children are not always listened to. It is easier to see them as clay to be moulded or blank slates to be written upon. Because of the dominant cultural messages (spun by an army of child development 'experts'), it is so easy to overprotect children, misinterpet their innocence and contain their spirit. So we worry about routines and sleep training, fear wildness and become anxious that they may not make the grade.

Yet researchers like Alison Gopnik tell us, contrary to the received wisdom of our developmental myths, that small children are really, really smart: *"babies and very young children know, observe, explore, imagine and learn more than we would ever have thought possible"*, she writes, *"In some ways, they are smarter than adults."*

Gopnik tells us that children see the world with an 'infant lantern', casting the light of awareness on the whole world around them. The 'adult spotlight', on the other hand, shines narrowly on those areas of experience we require for adult living. *"Consciousness narrows as a function of age"*, she writes, *"As we know more, we see less."* [85]

Allowing our child to teach us something is hard, and any activism carried out with love and soul is going to be difficult. It will always carry a tension between an ordinary life lived safely, and extraordinary potential lived with risk and passion.

Which do we want for our children? What do we want for ourselves?

We want both, of course; and therein lies the contradiction and the pain involved whenever deep love and soul are evoked. Soul making is not a convenient sort of activism – just a profoundly necessary one.

Interlude: Waiting for something

Today there was something I wanted to create. I don't know what it was, and I am waiting for it to emerge. When it comes, it will do so unbidden and untrammelled. It will have no cause and no causation.

It will be a spontaneous image bubbling up from somewhere deep. This is a counter-cultural claim. There must always a determinant – be it 'God' or history or genetics!

There is always a connection; always a relationship and pattern. There is always a reason – reductive and predictable – utilising one of the *'osophies* or *'ologies.* Yet this is not *my* truth as I sit, waiting for the spontaneity of this creative, poetic moment to emerge.

I try to force it; it will not come. I try to craft it and the clay turns to dust in my hands. I try to write my way into it and I create a piece – but not the piece that was waiting.

Each letter speaks, flies from the page. Each word floats off in a bubble or cloud. Each sentence meanders into itself; creates a flood-plain of meaning. Each poem encapsulates what was always there.

Wait. There it was. A fleeting image and I missed it.

Tomorrow I must wait again until I understand that the poetic image is (as Gaston Bachelard told us)[86] spontaneous and free unto itself. It materialises from below and travels as it pleases. It has no need of God or Science. The smallest poem is enough to contain it.

Part 6 notes and references

69. The last interview with Denis Potter before he died was with Melvyn Bragg on Channel 4, in March 1994. The full interview is available online at https://www.youtube.com/watch?v=XpnyPl8-ZcQ

70. *Presence: How to Use Positive Energy for Success in Every Situation* by Patsy Rodenburg (Michael Joseph, 2007).

71. *A Way of Being Free* by Ben Okri (Phoenix, 1998).

72. Interview with Radiohead in *Mojo Magazine* (Issue 171, February 2008).

73. Quote by Jerry Wennstrom from the film: *In the Hands of Alchemy,* which is about his life and his creative response to breakdown and the destruction of all his work until that point. You can find extracts from the film and more about his life and work at: http://www.handsofalchemy.com/default.htm

74. Quote from: *Burning the Candle* by Christine Evans, (Gomer Press, 2006).

75. *Crossing the Unknown Sea: Work as a Pilgrimage of Identity* by David Whyte (Riverhead, 2001).

76. Flow is a psychological state that is seen as 'optimal' for humans. It is experienced at the juncture when high demands meet high skill or capability, and is characterised by a sense of energetic immersion in an activity and of time passing almost unnoticed. It was proposed and developed by positive psychologist, Mahalyi Czsinsenkmahalyi. You can find out more in any of his books, in particular: *Flow: The Psychology of Happiness* (Rider, 2002).

77. *Outliers: the Story of Success* by Malcolm Gladwell (Penguin, 2009).

78. For an overview of mirror neurons and empathy see: *The Empathic Brain* by Christian Keysers (Social Brain Press, 2011)

79. *We Are The Ones We Have Been Waiting For* by Alice Walker (The New Press, 2006).

80. *Freedom Evolves* by Daniel Dennett (Penguin, 2004).

81. *Strength To Awaken: Make Strength Training Your Spiritual Practice and Find New Power and Purpose in Your Life* by Rob McNamara (Performance Integral, 2011).

82 *Beauty in Truth* is a film about Alice Walker's life and work. Further information can be found at: http://www.alicewalkerfilm.com/the-film.

83. *The Temple of My Familiar* by Alice Walker (Guild Press, 1989).

84. Quote from Andrew Taggart at: http://andrewjtaggart.com/2013/12/02/savoring-not-saving-the-world/. Andrew Taggart is a philosophical counselor, whose insightful online contemplations are always worth following. His website is: https://andrewjtaggart.com

85 Alison Gopnik is a researcher and writer in child psychology. She is the author of *The Scientist in the Crib: What Early Learning Tells Us About the Mind* (HarperCollins, 2001) and *The Philosophical Baby: What Children's Minds Tell Us about Truth, Love and the Meaning of Life* (Farrar, Straus and Giroux, 2009).

Interlude: Waiting for something

86. Gaston Bachelard was a French phenomenologist whose key work is *The Poetics of Space*, (Beacon Press, 1992), written in 1958, and translated into English in 1964. His introduction to this work is a succinct and stunning essay on creativity, psychology and soul. He writes: *"Later, when I shall have occasion to mention the relation of a new poetic image to an archetype lying dormant in the depths of the unconscious, I shall have to make it understood that this relation is not, properly speaking, a causal one. On the contrary: through the brllliance of an image, the distant past resounds with echoes, and it is hard to know at what depth these echoes will reverberate and die away. Because of its novely and its action, the poetic image has an entity and a dynamism of its own."* To emphasise the point he writes: *"...for the simple poetic image, there is no project; a flicker of the soul is all that is needed".*

Part 7
Small things and dangerous words

Alignment

the forces are aligning; opposition is inevitable –
political industrial financial versus artistic poetic resistance versus
rationalist materialist

the last child standing reads the manual and the healing –
the presence of the inevitable versus unpredictable integral versus creative
deep and crazy

numbers counting down in languages worth counting –
the wild waspish tang versus bland blue medication versus this blue fire

Dangerous words

Words are dangerous, but only if they carry truth that people don't want to hear. The best of these cut through the obscuring fogs of cultural decline and denial. The most effective face the reader with the mirror's reflection, then challenge us to conjure beauty from this stark glass. Such was the nature of the words of James Hillman, who died as I was finishing an early draft of this book.

Nothing he wrote was a compromise. His message carried difficult, dangerous beauty, that ran counter to the prevailing clinical and developmental paradigms of psychology. He championed imagination and reclaimed the soul as a living force within and outside us all. We are contained within soul, he told us, growing from acorns, reaching down into the rich loam of the world.

His was a world of myths and stories, metaphors and wildness. His was a psychology of deeply buried facets of soul, imagination and creativity, rooted in a world of mystery. He was dangerous because he championed depth and shadow precisely at the time our shallow culture invites us to fly into the sun.

Hillman became the greatest influence on my psychological thinking and therapeutic work. My discovery of his book, *'The Soul's Code'*,[87] in a little basement bookshop in Bloomsbury, was a changing point in my life. I devoured it avidly, and it gave shape to ideas and intuitions that had been brewing in my dreams and thinking for years.

Reading his rich, lucid prose was the closest I had been to an experience of revelation in literature and theory. *'The Soul's Code'* sits alongside Ursula Le Guin's magnificent, gentle opus, *'Always Coming*

Home',[88] as one of the two key books of my life. Like LeGuin's magical, swirling tales of future histories, Hillman's spirited writing imagines life back and forward, never settling for easy explanations of causation and determinism.

Nature and nurture are recognised phenomena, but only valid when lying firmly in the shadow of archetypal force. And in a culture in which easy answers and quick fixes are the order of the day, James Hillman emphasised the long life – deepening with time. He recognised the essentiality of pain and suffering as ways of listening to the deep life-breath of the wild earth and the raw city.

I did not know James Hillman, never met or worked with him, nor even saw him speak. Yet his wise, sometimes curmudgeonly voice lives on in his writings and recordings of his talks. His dangerous words remain to enrich and challenge us.

I will miss his presence in the world. I will take solace in his deep, secular parables of faith.

I will stand stock still in a field or a city street
as the wind or traffic whips around me,
and listen carefully for a whispered voice below the brisk noise.
His soul will be in grass and stone and sky.

Prophesies

In James Hillman's book of conversations and letters with Michael Ventura, his words read like prophesy.[89] He takes apart Western culture and the mirroring practices of modern psychotherapy. He shows how inadequate our human responses have been to the cultural, economic and ecological challenges that face us.

In that book, one letter stands out for me. It speaks of the need for us to face the forces that oppress us and threaten to destroy our world. To do this we must empty ourselves of certainty through a the political/spiritual process that Hillman called '*kenosis*'.

He writes: *"Kenosis puts the emptiness in a new light. It values emptiness. It says 'empty protest' is a via negativa, a non-positivist way of entering the political arena. You take your outrage seriously, but you don't force yourself to have answers".*

Finding answers is what politicians do; which is why they must always take action, make decisions, wage wars, make economic policy, take stances and take sides. *Kenosis* involves taking a psychological position in which we tell those who have failed us that we are no longer prepared to accept their certainty and solutions. *"Trust your nose"*, Hillman tells us, *"you know what stinks".*

I think that Hillman's task of soul-making may be more culturally suited to poets and activists, than therapists and psychologists. It is his clear integration of politics and imagination into psychology that distinguishes his approach from wannabe-scientists on the one hand, and head-in-the-clouds, spiritual gurus on the other. Indeed, in the arena of psychological development, he insists that self-help and individuation are less important than our living fully within the glorious, perilous *anima mundi* – the soul of the world. What makes his words essential is that they leave us with the psychological tools for human salvation, not simply personal transformation.

So Hillman's sharp words carry little sparks of hope. He tell us that if we strive deeply for justice and beauty, and follow our destiny with imagination and creativity, then perhaps we can be saved.

Life works like this

Happiness is not meant to be sustained; life doesn't work like that. One of the dangerous myths of our times is that some lifestyle, life-plan or life coach will help transform us. From the unhappy 'me' of yesterday, I will become the happy 'me' of tomorrow. In reality, there is little difference between the two. There is joy available in each moment, as there is pain and tragedy in every life.

Poet and soul philosopher, John O'Donohue wrote: *"There is no-one – regardless of how beautiful, sure, competent or powerful – that is not damaged internally in some way. Each one of us carries in our hearts the wound of mortality."* [90]

In each of us, there is a constant fluctuation between joy and pain, life and death, laughter and tears, freedom and belonging, love and hate. We push away the shadows and flames of existence, pretending that everything is bright and free.

"No wound is ever silent", as O'Donohue puts it, and even reading his words remind us of shadows. He died at the height of his powers, leaving memories and might-have-beens, alongside his words and deep wisdoms.

The illusion of sustainable happiness is particularly difficult for those who are in pain: those in mourning, those who are sick or waiting for the return of loved ones; those carrying the embodied memories of earlier abuse and trauma; those whose relationships are faltering.

For all of these people (who are, in reality, all of us) the illusion cannot be sustained. Sometimes, when we are in shadow, we look up at those who stand in sunlight, and feel shamed. We can't wait to be pulled to the surface; though when we get there, happiness can still elude us. We've been brought up too soon – the emotional equivalent of the 'bends'!

There is a real secret of joy that lies in accepting and being with ourselves and others with gentleness and compassion. And even in the midst of suffering, healing can be found in robust belly-laughter.

In her Observer column in October 2010, Victoria Coren remembered her father, comic writer Alan Coren: *"My dad once told me that if literary culture had to lose the complete works of Goethe or of PG Wodehouse, he reckoned it would be a lot worse off without Wodehouse. The older I get, the righter I think he was. This feels tender and important, because tomorrow is the third anniversary of my father's death. It's not the wisdom you miss most, it's the laughter."* [91]

Many psychotherapy clients are people courageous enought to acknowledge and talk about their vulnerability and woundedness to a total stranger. In these courageous conversations, the best moments often come when laughter bubbles up.

Sharing laughter can be a great, healing relief – and knowing that the best wisdoms are found in the simplest (and funniest) of places is another intuition worth having.

Resistance

Some people seem so obsessed with 'self' that they wish to be seen as self-less. Some also see their own enlightenment as integral to the Universe's evolution or 'God's plan'.

Yet true joy is found in the words and actions of those whose spirit emerges from another dimension entirely. They are beaten, imprisoned, ridiculed and oppressed for their ideals. Their inspiration is born out of self-knowledge and belonging, but emerges from the courage that make great acts of selflessness real.

"There are those who believe Black people possess the secret of joy," wrote Alice Walker, *"and that it is this that will sustain them through any spiritual or moral or physical devastation".*

In '*Possessing the Secret of Joy*', she writes of Tashi, a young woman whose childhood experience of circumcision in Africa defines her life and the lives of those who love her. Tashi's struggle with the brutalisation she suffered as a child gives substance to the ultimate joy that she and her people feel, even as she is executed by firing squad for the murder of her childhood tormentor. As she is about to die, a banner is unfurled for her to see: *"RESISTANCE IS THE SECRET OF JOY! it says in huge block letters".* [92]

And you can tell, from the afterword to this book, that Alice Walker herself was joyful in writing Tashi's painful story: *"Despite the pain one feels in honestly encountering the reality of life, I find it a wonderful time to be alive. This is because at no other time known to human beings has it been easier to give and receive energy, support and love from people never met, experiences never had".*

Alice Walker is an author who combines the self knowledge that deep therapy brings, with the searing awareness that comes from being at the heart of the African-American political and cultural struggle.

For her, the shadows have often been as real and material as metaphorical. She understands that joy and pain go together – that real joy comes when pain is faced and struggled with. She knows there is no easy path to enlightenment.

In the book, Tashi has been devastated by her experiences, yet ultimately these give meaning to who she is. They make possible her final, courageous and enlightened explosion of joy in the last moment of her life: *"There is a roar as if the world cracked open and I flew inside. I am no more. And satisfied."*

Emptying out

In another story, Michael Ventura remembered a bleak childhood: *"When those memories of sexual abuse started coming up for me – which happened like clockwork on my fortieth birthday – after about a month of car crashes and black holes, I went to a therapist. He was an old man, a Jungian. I was going on and on about the abuse and about my mother, and he sort of smiled and said, "You know, what's happened to you, it forged your connection with the soul's mysteries didn't it? And that's what you write about isn't it? Would you rather have been writing about something else?"*[93]

One cultural belief is that we shouldn't be owning up to suffering at all. Another (paradoxically) has it that we become defined by our victimhood. Yet when we listen to a person who is suffering, they put us exquisitely in touch with the existential realities of life. They guide us – challenging us to oppose the forces that cause the problem – to become activists for joy. For those who have suffered, joy cannot emerge by being defined, constrained or paralysed by suffering. It can only become real through transcendence and resistance.

In his conversations with Ventura, James Hillman talks of the need for an *"emptying out of certainty"*. If we have learned anything in recent times, it is that certainty has failed us. Bankers, politicians and leaders, whose raison d'etre is the appearance of certainty, have become our culture's professional narcissists. They look in the mirror, seeing only good things, as the world heats up and the economy melts down.

We are not blameless. We still allow brutalisation in the name of the civilisations these men deem to rule. However, we can withdraw our permission from the people who keep up this destruction. We can do this by accepting uncertainty and unknowing for ourselves.

Finding joy in resistance is a tricky business. In giving up the safety of our projected self, there is the possibility that empying out could mean our death. However, Nelson Mandela, Mahatma Ghandi, Martin Luther-King, Aung San Suu Kyi and others could not have inspired us, had they not been prepared to give up their life and freedom for the resistence – and to risk the pain of struggle.

Following their example, new archetypes of hope and joy can be reborn. These will emerge both from suffering and emptying out as Hillman and Ventura describe. Tentative answers will be reached for and arrived at. However, the wisdom of history tells us that 'liberators' must always be vigilant; to avoid becoming new sources of suffering and destruction.

We are not angry enough

We are often told that we have to be 'in the moment' in order to be happy; yet while we sit and meditate, evolve and transcend, people are dying, the planet crumbles, species become extinct. It suits those in power – desperately trying to keep things as they are – for us to keep searching for happiness. The more content we can be, the longer they are able to keep things as they are. So we need to get angrier. Angrier with ourselves, and angrier with the cultures we have collaborated with and created.

First, I will keep the spirit, but discard the spiritual.

We won't change the world by enlightening ourselves; we need to be authentically, honestly angry. We have neglected the shadows for so long that they have a nihilistic life of their own. It's time to learn the art of anger so we can gentle these forces in ourselves. Now that would be an emotional intelligence to contend with!

So, first be furious, but don't lash out. Don't turn your anger into self pity or self destruction. Never choose despair. Learn how to channel and change. Have angry conversations that are fierce with love. Have rage that lights up the soul. Don't get lost in regret or turn anger to shame. Douse yourself in self compassion – then ignite!

Now cast your anger into the world. Find the right targets. Never ignore suffering. Suffer with the world, if you need to, but don't give in to it. Stand up to the blind leaders of our destruction, and do not accept their justifications and appeasements. Have rage that lights up the world and don't jump to the challenge to find solutions. Go to places where you are not expected or welcome – and make a stand.

I will embark on the project, and discard the projection.

Being righteously and rightfully angry is a necessity of our time. We have lost the art of anger. We believe it to be wrong. We are told that it must be tempered and managed. We see anger as the opposite of love, when it is, in fact, its essential companion. Only when we feel love and rage, one and the same time, and can face each other with courage and tenderness, will we have a chance for freedom and true redemption.

Only then will I sit with God's still small voice, and be satisfied.

Reconcile the written word

David Abram wrote that the advent of the written word distanced humankind from the earth. The spread of writing and reading extracted us spatially and sensually from the living world. By making our words symbolic, we lost the magical animism that our ancestors took for granted: *"it is only when a culture shifts its participation to those printed letters that the stones fall silent."* [94]

Once upon a time, storytelling was an embodied act of connection. Now human stories are two-dimensional tales, evoked by printed marks on a flat page. Once, stories were circular; endless cycles of space-time embedded in the myths of ancient, oral cultures. Storytelling was a repetitive ritual of 'now'. We gathered round an evening fire, on a plain or in the depths of a forest. We were surrounded by the animals, plants and places we sang and dreamed of. Now stories are linear, with a beginning, middle and an end.

We start a book and finish it – revisiting a story only if it evokes something deep. We write only of humans and their concerns. And time moves forward.

The written word might have disconnected us from the wild, yet it has civilised us in other ways. The uncomfortable truth about the wilderness is that it is unpleasant and brutal. To survive, our nomad ancestors had to be cruel to match and surpass our fellow predators' propensity to be red in tooth and claw. The wilderness recognises no separation between hunter and the hunted, and so the human psyche was one with the world. This inherent cruelty remained with us as we settled and became 'civilised' in our villages, towns and cities.

The page turned again on this human story and ideas were written down. The written word enabled writer and the reader to connect in a way that had not been possible before. And crucially, the written story – with it's complexity and metaphorical possibilities – allows empathy and equality. *"If I understand your suffering"*, says the liberated reader, *"then I am less likely to brutalise you"*. This is Steven Pinker's message: humans are less violent, he says, and it is, in part, because of our democratised literacy.[95]

We might bring the argument full circle. If it wasn't for the empathy that the written word holds in potential, we would not have reached this stage in our thinking. We can now see the earth and our fellow creatures as being worthy of fellowship and nurture; not just to be exploitated. The written word carries a promise of our salvation and re-imagination of a future in which renewed connections can be sustained.

When I first read David Abram's dissection of the linguistic and temporal sources of our separation from the world, I realised he was describing phenomena I had experienced since childhood. The separation of time-space, body-mind, voice-world, always felt unnatural to me. My reveries are physical and imaginative. My words evoke pictures and places. My memories conflate with what might be. In dreams all this comes together: stories of humanity encapsulated in the written word, embodied in my physicality.

I am drawn to the Dreamtime. If I believed I could sing, I would have sung *all* my journeys.

A walk in the woods

When I told people I was going for a walk in the woods to talk about joy, I did get some raised eyebrows. The people who know me have long considered that my enthusiasms take me to some pretty odd places. They also know that, within the confines of my therapy rooms, some extraordinary people are psychologically very courageous, and that I sometimes have a way of helping them reclaim their necessary resilience and vulnerability.

However, even balanced, open and joyful people sometimes find it hard to openly contemplate ideas such as soul, spirit and even beauty. Even they can be ambivalent towards meditation or talking about their feelings – or going for a walk in the woods to talk about joy.

Why is this? What peculiar cultural forces are at work that mean we are more comfortable laughing off joy as the province of the decidedly flaky, than toughing it out and saying: *"yes, I'm proud of my curiosity, vulnerability and sensitivity"*? Why do people turn away from the promise of a good conversation for fear of being considered a bit of a 'wuss'? This is a small but significant cultural challenge that we face!

I guess it was their loss, because this walk in the woods was genuinely joyful. The day will stay in my memory as a touchstone moment in my mid-life. The journey down on the train was comfortable and fun. The two hours of solitude gave me time to think, to enjoy music, watch a short film and read a bit. This was the spade work for my meeting with my friend, who in his own life's journey, has learned to love gardening and the growth of gentle knowing.

My arrival and our meeting marked the beginning of a conversation that rose and fell through the forest, throughout that day.

My friend, Patrick, held the map, the direction and destination. I allowed him this and enjoyed the freedom. He also held the silence, for which, in my talkative excitement, I was also grateful.[96]

At his bidding, we stopped from time to time. He would invite me to notice a tree, a glade, a view from a bridge or a transitory place. He would pause and draw attention to birdsong, a woodpecker at work, the momentary silence.

Then, a break for a meal, some practical, spirited business, and back into the woods for our return.

Loving the small things

A great joy of relationship is meeting someone with whom you have a conversation that flows; with whom important things are communicated in natural ways. Someone you feel safe enough with to offer something precious to. That day I trusted my friend's acceptance of me. I felt sure enough in my own vulnerability, to allow creativity and spirit to flow from deep soul and shared meaning.

One of the great joys of a walk in the woods (or on a moor, cliff or mountain path) is a reminder to us that there is so much more to existence than human aspiration and thought.

There is a whole world out there, full of life, one that has no regard for our strange and unimportant human concerns. However much we strive to be seen, search for meaning or climb ladders of career and achievement, there is still a tree in the forest that has been there for a thousand years, and a woodpecker that taps out its strange calling card with no apparent recognition of our presence.

Naturalist Edward O. Wilson touched on this when writing of Henry Thoroux's '*Walden*': *"A thousand years will pass and Walden Woods will stay the same, I think, a flickering equilibrium that works its magic on human emotion in variations with each experience."* [97]

Wilson is a lifelong, ancient naturalist of the tribe he calls the *"lovers of little things"*: mini-beasts, insects, worms and scuttling things that makes up most of the animal life on our planet. He also knows something of the humility of a walk in the woods: *"we stand up to go a-sauntering"*, he writes; joyfully anticipating his own imagined conversation with Theroux – and with the forest itself.

My own walk in the woods took me from the worldly concerns of a modern life, down the tracks, through the gateway to the forest; then (for a short while) into the realms of human joy.

This was joy that grew from solitude, companionship, friendship, conversation, and from being in a beautiful and soulful world – full of slow, poetic magic – that is always there for us, if we are prepared to be open to it.

From the wild

I live in a place where we are never too far away from wildness. This is not wilderness – we have none of the giant plains and canyons of northern America – more a series of micro-wild environments and ecosystems in which humans, animals and elements co-exist in close proximity. The landscape dominates and human survival here is aided by stoicism, wellington boots and four-wheel drive vehicles. However, the birds, in particular, have more subtle and adaptive relationships with the place that we can only watch and admire.

The clever crows on the cliff tops imitate the hawks in the way they hold their position and speed into the eddying winds. The buzzards and kites, in their turn, find and hold their mark and stand stark still above the saturated winter fields. And the peregrines seem to control and harness the wind itself, accelerating into a breathless parallel dimension.

Beneath the gaze of these predators, their prey scurries and busies itself: clouds of pigeons and starlings, flurries of winter finches, rabbits, mice and weasels. Foxes and badgers skirt the fields and muddy roads in search of their own quarry. Robins and wrens peck and hop around the margins of our habitation. Beneath it all, the small things of Edward Wilson's passion lattice the ground, unseen by all but the most observant of us humans.

In winter, it seems wilder here than ever. The west wind is relentless; driving the rain into the squat stone barns and houses. In spring, the colours will emerge, breathtaking and beautiful, and the sky – like the creatures who fly in it – will seems to breath out and expand.

What can we make of such a place? We are human, and this is an impressive thing. Yet, the wildness around us tells us that we are little more than animals with big brains and noisy engines. Much more impressive, therefore, is the human who understands that she is animal! The realisation of this, and the communication of this contemplation, is the truly creative part of being a human being.

And this is the well from which all truly creative acts spring. It is why the more self-consciously ambitious a human project is, the more sterile and limited it becomes. Human grandiosity takes us far from our grounded nature, and focuses our attention on the driven desperation of doing.

As Andrew Taggart asks us: *"How did we go from a conception of human beings as, at their best, contemplative animals to one in which they are creatures who act for the sake of getting things done?"* [98]

Being intimate with wildness makes such grandiosity impossible, and puts us back in touch with the cycles of being. And, perhaps, sitting with the experience of the wind and rain and the hawks and swirling starlings, might make it more likely that when something is done, it will be creative, grounded and worthwhile.

The human in me

Being human is sometimes hard. Our problems lie in just being human, and the symptoms of this are over-thinking, analysis, emotionalisation and a desperation to make meaning from our lives. There are times, however, when it is enough just to be in the world. As Mary Oliver tells us: *"You only have to let the soft animal of your body love what it loves."* [99]

One winter's day: *A dog on the beach played mischievously with his owner – dashing off and returning, dashing off and returning. A string of crows passed overhead, riding the winds and air currents. A surfer, clad black like a seal, paddled out against white waves. I, clad in a warm brown coat, like some kind of a shambling, beach bear, walked along the falling tideline and felt like a soft animal; furred up against the biting onshore wind.*

It is hard to keep these intuitions clean. All too soon the human in me returns. Things to do. Gifts to buy and food to make. Relationships to maintain. Work to think about. Money to earn. Meaning to be made.

Don't get me wrong, I love the human in me. He gives me an appreciation of the world's beauty, helps me love and inspires me so I can write these words. But I have often wished I could be the animal at will – to be free from anxious striving.

Now, living my life backwards, I come to a realisation about why I studied Zoology years back. I sometimes retain the intuition of a naturalist who knows that he is one of the flock, but does not want to just a part of the herd; and I have always been fascinated with systems and ecologies within which lifeforms live.

Ecology matters, and I now use this awareness to try to understand the difference between political and natural belonging.

Birds, animals and species of trees, for example, are not natives of countries with human-given names, borders and nationalities, but denizens of lands and continents boundaried by seas and streams, hedges, ridges and mountain ranges. The sea currents, breezes, water flows and valleys carved by ice, provide the topography for the nations of the wilderness.

Such a realisation demands a new form of belonging: a new politics of earth; one based on new, natural borders and requiring more than one species to have a voice. If we are to move away from purely human constructions – gods, symbols, numbers, words – towards this more holistic perspective, we will also require a new diplomacy of the wilderness that recognises the logic of evolution and the forces that shape our world.

It will not be for politicians. The naturalist or ecologist working in the field, observing – just observing – is the activist with the best chance of understanding these deep connections – the artist and poet too.

The three-fold self

Let's say for the sake of simplicity that all human beings throughout history have been born to operate in the realms of three selves.[100]

The first is the fundamental soul self, containing all our deepest talents, virtues and destinies: *"In each of us, there is a little voice that knows exactly which way to go,"* [101] said Alice Walker.

This is soul: it encapsulates the me-nesses of me and the you-nesses of you. It is has different names in different traditions – soul, inheritance, core-self, true-self, strengths, virtues, calling, *daemon.* Soul is not a singular self, but is connected – through metaphor, poetic image, evolution and archetype – beneath the surface of our lives and waking awareness to all other souls.

The second is a social self of learned behaviour, culture, human belonging, relationship and interpersonal habits. It is in our relationships and how we learn to love. It is embedded in psychological theories of development and attachment and the assumptions we make about the determinism of nurture. It is in the narcissism we bring to world and our habits of avoidance. It is in our families and our connections. It is in the love we hold for others and the limits of the true love we hold for ourselves.

This social self dominates contemporary human consciousness, culture, motivation and behaviour. For better or worse, for richer or poorer, the social, relational self is one marriage we recognise!

Third, and least acknowledged (but inherent to the 'self' of indigenous peoples), is the ecological self that emerges from the material world.

This emerges from the phenomena of night and day, dark and light, body and mind, hill and forest, sea and land, big sky and deep waters. This 'self' is not a real self at all, but a constellation of ever-changing experience of life on a shape-shifting earth.

This realm of self holds a sense of presence and connection that dissolves the boundaries between the human world and nature, and puts our small human concerns in perspective. In a way, this is a self of everythingness – more gritty and grounded than transcendent.

Each human culture has had its own dynamic balance between these three. Something is lost if a culture becomes blind to any of these dimensions. Our own civilisation, and the psychology it has developed to explain its mind, is fixated with the social self to the extent that the other two – soul and ecology of mind – scarcely get a look in. This partly explains why we have got into the mess we are in, and why we still find it so hard to create the solutions that may, even at this late stage, be possible.

We have a one-track mindset, so to speak, that is obsessed with social aspects of human functioning. As a result, we find it almost impossible to locate the other two dimensions in meaningful or sustainable ways; and most people believe that they are unhappy because they cannot get their life 'right' in the narrow realm of the social self.

My sense is that it is more because we live our lives too narrowly; attenuating the richness of soul, connection and ecology into a yearning for self development, recognition and relationship. Wishing for something – perfect love – that can never be fully realised.

Facing storms

It is calm now. This past winter we've had weeks of storms and tidal surges; our local beach was trashed; the sea defences breached and the valley behind – along with the pub and beach shop – flooded.

Each night we lay in our bedroom in the eaves of the house, separated from ferocious wind and rain by only a skylight. After each battering, the rain would blow over, the night sky reveal itself – breathtaking and bright – only for another band of storm clouds to race in from the west.

This is winter in west Wales, but it reminds us of the challenges we face globally. The world and its weather are not benign and benevolent much of the time, and we humans – like all other creatures – have to struggle for survival. The difference is that for civilised humans survival is no longer an everyday concern. We take it for granted that we can thrive (not just survive) in our insulated homes and electricity-fed and digitally-driven lives.

The patterns of technology and consumption that most of us now live within (even in remote areas of the world), have distanced us inexorably from the networks that nature has sustained for most of our history. Now, as we lie awake at night, we might only be a few inches away from the storm, but unless we are personally affected by the destruction, it might as well be just another news item from across the world.

The psychology of this is insidious. What has crept into the modern human mind is a kind of mental insulation; a layer of plasticised wadding that keeps out the cold and wet.

We have become blasé about our ability to live, shop and consume; to eat what we want when we want; to drive where we want when we want. If we were to face up to the reality of what storms might mean, we'd have to accept fear, despair, and uncertainty –something few of us seem prepared to do these days. We are insulated from death, isolation and meaninglessness by the trappings and habits of civilisation.

Each year we shore ourselves up against these existential storms with New Year's resolutions: shutting out the challenge of the present with fantasies of a better, fitter, slimmer, richer, more successful year to come.

Here's an emerging truth. By the end of the century, according to the latest climate change research, the world will have warmed to temperatures that lie at the very top-end of envisaged global warming scenarios, with serious – perhaps even catastrophic – environmental and social consequences.[102]

Who is facing this? Who is even acknowledging this? What kind of world will my little granddaughters live in? What kind of networks and patterns will enable them to survive and thrive? What are we going to do about it?

Perhaps it has all gone too far, and all we can now do is to learn ways of living with the consequences. I want to be hopeful; but I recognise that, in the face of storms, all you can sometimes do is batten the hatches and hunker down for the long winter to come.

A final story

I have always held and cherished two values as truth.

First, that the collective human spirit is wonderful and has the potential to change the world. In this view, human development – advancement – lies in community and love. Second, that individual freedom of thought, action and self-hood is fundamental to humans. Our wellbeing, sanity and self-hood lies in our subjective experience of uniqueness in each of us.

Yet, both carry paradox – and shadow.

The collective spirit can bring hate, as well as love; even the totalitarian demand that we 'belong'. Community can be oppressive, even when it sets out to nurture and liberate. And evil can be born out of a twisted desire to prove that we are part of the crowd.

Likewise, individual autonomy can lead not just to freedom but to inequality, selfishness and the fantasy of self-made, 'man-as-an-island'. Individuality is distorted with the ego's fantasy, and this narcissistic cultural norm can flow like poison into a disregard for anyone or anything other than our 'self'.

Caught in the shadows, we fret and weep over trivial concerns and minor tragedies close to home, yet turn our faces from far greater ills, disasters and cruelties bestowed on the earth and its inhabitants. We love those close to us – and this brings us joy – but fail to take our love beyond these enclosures, into the world and the wild.

The biggest problem with these values is that they are human. The collective only includes people. Freedom is only a human privilege. What is missed is a wider commonwealth and a wilder freedom that once were found in the identification of 'self' with the earth and our nurturance of other lifeforms around us.

What remains? These deep, human birthrights: nesting and embedding; belonging and freedom; connection and subjectivity; love and self experienced as imaginative, poetic image; and real development – individuals in step with their calling and communities joined in cooperation and care.

To be hopeful – we can do this thing! All we may need to do is to 're-mind' ourselves. We were once animals with big minds; we just need to re-grow them.

We, social animals who can love with passion and breadth.
We, creatures of ecology, whose soft bodies are embedded in the patterns and energies on the earth.
We, soulful animals, born with purpose and startling individuality.

And so the task of soul-making is also one of 'self-minding' – finding a way for each of the small rills and runnels of our lives to join with the great, wide rivers of our world, and to empty out – at the end of days – into the deep expanse of ocean.

And this will always be a great story to tell!

Part 7 notes and references

87. *The Soul's Code: In Search of Character and Calling*, by James Hillman (cited above).

88. *Always Coming Home* by Ursula LeGuin (cited above).

89. *We've Had a Hundred Years of Psychotherapy and the World's Getting Worse* by James Hillman and Michael Ventura (HarperSanFrancisco, 1993).

90. *Eternal Echoes: Exploring Our Hunger To Belong* by John O'Donohue, (Bantam, 2000).

91. Victoria Coren writing in *The Observer* (17/10./2010) at: http://www.theguardian.com/commentisfree/2010/oct/17/victoria-coren-nick-clegg-greer-jacobson

92. *Possessing the Secret of Joy* by Alice Walker (Vintage, 1993).

93. *We've had a Hundred Years of Psychotherapy and the World's Getting Worse* by James Hillman and Michael Ventura (cited above).

94. *The Spell of the Sensuous: Perception and Language in a More-Than-Human World* by David Abram (Vintage, 1997) is one of the great books of the end of the twentieth century, and maps out a soul of our times. Based on phenomenology and beautifully written, Abram shows where the human ecological mind has been lost and where it can be found again. His second book, *Becoming Animal: An Earthly Cosmology* (Vintage, 2011) continues the theme of how the wild can be part of us again.

95. *The Better Angels of Our Nature: The Decline of Violence In History And Its Causes* by Steven Pinker (Penguin, 2012)

96. Patrick Andrews is an ex-corporate lawyer, who now works as an activist and advisor in sustainability and development. He is good at holding things – spaces, people and ideas. He blogs at: https://medium.com/@patrickandr

97. *The Future of Life* by Edward O. Wilson (Abacus, 2003).

98. *Visions of Being Human: Contemplation and Action* by Andrew Taggart, blog post at: http://andrewjtaggart.com/2012/12/26/visions-of-being-human-contemplation-and-action/

99. Quote from poem: *Wild Geese* by Mary Oliver in *Dream Work* (Atlantic Monthly Press, 1996).

100. The 'three-fold self' is an integral model I have developed for my *21Soul* development project and e-course. You can find out more at: http://www.21soul.co.uk

101. Alice Walker was interviewed in *The Guardian* (9/3/2013) on the recent film, *Beauty in Truth*, about her life and work. Further information about the film is at: http://www.alicewalkerfilm.com/the-film. The interview can be found at: http://www.theguardian.com/books/2013/mar/09/alice-walker-beauty-in-truth-interview

102. This is based on reports and discussions around the Intergovernmental Panel on Climate Change (IPCC) report: *Climate Change 2014: Impacts, Adaptation and Vulnerability* (IPCC, 2014). The scientific models and data around man-made climate change are constantly being refined and updated, and can be tracked on the IPCC website: http://ipcc.ch

Steve Thorp

Steve Thorp is an integral practitioner and writer. He works with individuals, groups and organisations to support soul-making and cultures of deep wellbeing. In the past he has worked as a teacher, psychotherapist, consultant and activist. You can find out more about his work at: **www.21soul.co.uk**.

Dedications and thanks

(updated 2018)

For Mary, Jenny, Sarah and Ruth, who are always with me and keep me from being too serious, For Freya and Ellie my grandchildren, who remind me of the unconditionality of love and the mysterious originality of soul.

For my Mum, Win, who died this year, and my Dad, Ian, who loved her so dearly for so many years.

For Michael Soth, who has, for many years, guided my *"unfolding, unnoticed, neglected soul"*, providing solace, wisdom and challenge along the way.

For friends and collaborators whose good words have found ways into my creative life. For clients and conversation partners, whose insight and courage has touched and inspired me.

Raw Mixture Publishing

What readers are saying:

"Soul Manifestos and Pieces of Joy is amazing, extraordinary, powerful, necessary and deeply inspiring", *(Dave Hicks, author of Educating for Hope in Troubled Times, 2014).*

"I think this book is going to stay with me forever. The kind of book that I will pick up and read sections, pick up and immerse myself in. The balance and purity make me calm and yet excite me at the same time…I read the page on Childhood and welled up – I think it is a wonderfully written, thought provoking marvel". *(Dawn J on Facebook).*

"Really lovely and so inspiring – a wonderful book indeed. There is something beautiful on every page" *(reader review on the People's Book Prize 2016 website).*

"A brilliant book by Steve Thorp and important for our times" *(reader review on the People's Book Prize 2016 website).*

"…I'd love to recommend this book to you...It's absolutely beautifully written & the perfect antidote to the hustle & bustle of modern life – especially if you're feeling frazzled, lost or just in need of a moment of inner peace or reflection. Don't worry, I'm not going all Guru on you – but I love it and thought you might too" *(Charlie D on Facebook).*

"I'm reading a couple of pieces each day and I'm really enjoying it. It's been thought provoking, comforting, baffling and inspirational! Not all at the same time obviously! It's chock full of good stuff" *(Phil L).*

"Am enjoying Soul Manifestos and Pieces of Joy. Definitely a soulful read". *(Matt F on Twitter).*